W9-DGS-349

HOMELESSNESS IN
GLOBAL PERSPECTIVE

SOCIAL ISSUES IN GLOBAL PERSPECTIVE

David Levinson
Melvin Ember

General Editors

The *Social Issues in Global Perspective* series is prepared under the auspices and with the support of the Human Relations Area Files at Yale University. HRAF, the foremost international research organization in the field of cultural anthropology, is a not-for-profit consortium of twenty-two sponsoring members and 300 participating member institutions in twenty-five countries. The HRAF archive, established in 1949, contains nearly one million pages of information on the cultures of the world.

HOMELESSNESS IN GLOBAL PERSPECTIVE

Irene Glasser

G.K. HALL & CO.
An Imprint of Macmillan Publishing Company
NEW YORK

Maxwell Macmillan Canada
TORONTO

Maxwell Macmillan International
NEW YORK OXFORD SINGAPORE SYDNEY

Excerpt from "Hard Travelin'" (p. 13). Words and music by Woody Guthrie. TRO–©
Copyright 1959 (Renewed), 1964 (Renewed) Ludlow Music, Inc., New York, NY. Used by
permission.

Copyright © 1994 by Human Relations Area Files, Inc.

All rights reserved. No part of this book may be reproduced or transmitted in any form
or by any means, electronic or mechanical, including photocopying, recording, or by any
information storage and retrieval system, without permission in writing from the
Publisher.

G.K. Hall & Co.   Maxwell Macmillan Canada, Inc.
An Imprint of Macmillan Publishing Company   1200 Eglinton Avenue East
866 Third Avenue   Suite 200
New York, NY 10022   Don Mills, Ontario M3C 3N1

Macmillan Publishing Company is part of the Maxwell Communication Group of
Companies.

Library of Congress Catalog Card Number: 93-25087

Printed in the United States of America

Printing number
1 2 3 4 5 6 7 8 9 10

Library of Congress Cataloging-in-Publication Data

Glasser, Irene.
    Homelessness in global perspective / Irene Glasser.
        p. cm. — (social issues in global perspective)
    Includes bibliographical references and index.
    ISBN 0-8161-7379-6 (alk. paper). — ISBN 0-8161-1606-7 (pbk. : alk. paper)
    1. Homelessness. I. Title. II. Series.
HV4493.G53 1994   93-25087
362.5—dc20   CIP

The paper used in this publication meets the minimum requirements of American
National Standard for Information Sciences—Permanence of Paper for Printed Library
Materials. ANSI Z39.48-1984. ∞ ™

LIBRARY
ALMA COLLEGE
ALMA, MICHIGAN

For my loving family,
My parents, Charlotte and Gerald Biederman,
My sons, Jason, Raphael, Jonathan, and Nathaniel,
My husband, Morty

Contents

Acknowledgments

In writing a book from a world perspective, one must rely on the expertise of many people, especially since much of the world literature on homelessness either is not found in published sources or is referenced in less than obvious ways. I wish here to thank some of the many people who helped me in this rather large undertaking.

First, I would like to thank David Levinson, vice-president of Human Relations Area Files, Inc., for inviting me to write about homelessness in global perspective. I have appreciated his guidance at every step along the way.

I would like to thank my colleagues throughout the world who have assisted me in locating homelessness materials. These include Pertti J. Pelto, Pam Hunte, Josef Gugler, Susan Hutson, Michael Cernea, Gretel Pelto, M. Shah, Hydie Sobel, and the agencies Childhope and Child Workers Concerned of Nepal.

I am grateful for a sabbatic leave from Eastern Connecticut State University in fall 1992 that enabled me to finish this project.

The Connecticut State University Research Foundation awarded me a grant for the translation of works on homelessness into English from Chinese, Portuguese, German, Danish, and French sources. I thank Zibin Guo, Xun Wang, Jorge Cervera, Hannah Clements, and Solvej Jensen, et un très spécial merci à ma chère mère, Charlotte Biederman.

The Eastern Connecticut State University Library, especially its interlibrary loan department, has been an excellent resource throughout this project. I would especially like to thank Erna Luering, Jody Newmyer, Marguerite Rauch, A. Stanley-Gorling, and Catherine Tyl.

The Canadian Studies Program at Eastern Connecticut State University was helpful in providing me with assistance to research aspects of homelessness in Canada. I would like to especially thank Leon Sarin and John St. Onge for their help. I would also like to thank Norman T. London, Academic Relations Officer of the Canadian Embassy, and John McNeil, Academic Relations Officer, Canadian Consulate General in New York, for their support in pursuing Canadian research.

For their encouragement of my ongoing interest in homelessness under the umbrella of Eastern Connecticut State University, I would like to thank President David G. Carter, Vice-President Dimitrios Pachis, Director of Fiscal Affairs John S. Berkett, and Sociology Chairman, Robert J. Wolf.

I was fortunate to have the excellent assistance of Kathleen DelMonte, sociology and anthropology student at Eastern Connecticut State University.

I would like to acknowledge the permissions I received to use the photographs of homeless people from UNICEF (United Nations Children's Emergency Fund), UNHCR (United Nations High Commissioner for Refugees), the Museum of the City of New York, and Sandy Hale. I am grateful to Susan Hutson and Mark Liddiard for their permission to use the Homeless Careers Chart.

I would like to thank my aunt and uncle, Esther and Morris Biederman, for their enthusiasm for this project, and their support of me, always.

I would like to thank Catherine Carter and Jane Andrassi at Macmillan for their thorough and helpful editorial assistance.

1
Introduction

At age ten, Enrique had been in the streets less than a year when I met him. Originally he attributed his deformed hand and severely scarred arm to a terrible bus accident in which he was injured and both his parents were killed. Later, in a quiet, collected manner, he told his true story. When his family first arrived in Cali, Enrique had accompanied his mother as she begged on the streets. Then gradually he had begun to beg alone, returning home each evening—to a piece of canvas stretched over a wooden frame, underneath a city street overpass. "One night I came back, and there was another family there. They said my family left at midday. I don't know where they went. So now I live with the other boys on the street. But I'm not alone." There had been no bus accident: Enrique's deformed hand was a birth defect; his scar the result of a beating. (Felsman 1981:43)

Joe and Mary were both in their sixties and drank much of the day. They were often at the soup kitchen, he loudly playing the tunes of an earlier era on the piano in the dining room. When someone occasionally asked him to quiet down, he would curse at them. Mary, thin and fragile looking, was often bleeding from wounds on her legs or arms sustained from falls.

In September they were evicted from their room in the hotel, where they had lived together for three years. The manager evicted them because of the smell emanating from their room and the fire hazard caused by an accumulation of things. On the day they were evicted, Joe had a black eye and stitches on his face. He had fallen off the sidewalk when the grocery cart which he used for support when walking had slipped away. (Glasser 1991:27)

From a street child in Colombia to an elderly alcoholic couple on the streets of the United States, homelessness is an issue that commands our attention in the last decade of the twentieth century. This book addresses the issue of homelessness from a global perspective.

There is no organized "world homelessness literature." In writing this book, I have created a world homelessness literature based on the published and nonpublished literature on homelessness found in scholarly research, community participation projects, governmental reports, and newspapers. Whenever possible I have chosen literature written by scholars and community activists who are natives of the culture or country under study in order to avoid applying ethnocentric standards from one culture to another. However, rarely are the authors of the research themselves homeless, though there are some exceptions (see *Child of the Dark: The Diary of Carolina Maria De Jesus* 1963). In addition, many of the researchers, even if from the country of study, are from a culture group other than those of the homeless themselves (see Hardoy and Satterthwaite 1989).

Various points of view (one might say biases) are reflected in the literature on homelessness. Governments may underestimate homelessness and concentrate on a few exemplary housing improvement schemes; nongovernmental organizations may have religious or political agendas that pervade their writing; and newspapers and television news coverage may gravitate toward the most dramatic and muckraking stories.

The research on which this book is based covers all regions of the world. Although most of the literature consulted was in English, I have also used articles and reports translated from Spanish, French, Portuguese, Danish, German, and Chinese.

A major limitation of any survey of homelessness is that many homeless people, whether living on the street or in the most meager shelter, either have not been or cannot be studied and written about, and therefore are not known to us. Why do studies from various parts of the world exist or not exist? The answer may have to do with the varying number of scholars (and their priorities) within a given country, the financial support of the government, voluntary agencies, or academia, or it may be that research does exist but its results are not shared.

Perhaps the greatest value in a global survey is the possibility of garnering the best of the solutions to homelessness from every corner of the world. Although programs and policies that address homelessness cannot be transplanted totally from culture to culture without some alterations, there are many ideas that can work outside their local context.

The Concept of Homelessness

As a concept, homelessness takes on a variety of meanings and understandings as we move from one culture to another. For example, the occupants of a one-room house constructed of mud and wattle (sticks, twigs, and branches) that is a great improvement over the makeshift "igloos" of cardboard, branches, and plastic of a squatter settlement in Nairobi, Kenya (Settlements Information Network Africa 1986b), would be classified as homeless in most parts of the industrialized world. Major definitional differences of homelessness exist not only in moving between developing and industrialized nations, but also within these broad categories themselves. For example, two or more families sharing a small apartment (out of necessity rather than desire) may be termed the "doubled-up homeless" in the United States (see Ropers 1988), whereas shelter sharing has been a pervasive and generally accepted practice in Moscow (see Kudryavtse 1986) until an apartment can be found by the second family.

There have been several attempts at a generic definition of homelessness and, inversely, of adequate shelter. A widely quoted definition of homelessness is suggested by Caplow, Bahr, and Sternberg (1968): "Homelessness is a condition of detachment from society characterized by the absence or attenuation of the affiliative bonds that link settled persons to a network of interconnected social structures" (494).

As we shall see, this "detachment definition" applies to much of the traditional research about homeless men, primarily in the United States and England. But it does not apply to pavement-dwelling families, or to the hundreds of thousands of people living in squatter settlements throughout the world. It may even have limited application to the homeless men who have been shown to maintain "affiliative bonds" within their own subculture. However, despite its limitations, the single man, alone, sleeping on the street over a subway grate, is the mental image that is most often conjured up by the word "homeless."

Like the term "homelessness," adequate shelter is also difficult to define. In 1987 representatives from forty countries representing fifty-seven nongovernmental organizations met in Limuru, Kenya, to address homelessness and poverty. There, they issued the Limuru Declaration, which speaks of a basic standard of shelter:

> Adequate, affordable shelter with basic services is a fundamental right of all people. Governments should respect the right of all people to shelter, free from the fear of forced eviction or removal, or the threat of their home being demolished. . . .
>
> Adequate shelter includes not only protection from the elements, but also sources of potable water in or close to the house, provision for the removal of household and human liquid and solid wastes, site drainage, emergency life-saving services, and easy access to health care. In urban centres, a house site within easy reach of social and economic opportunities is also an integral part of an adequate shelter. (Turner 1988:187)

In addition to security of tenure, potable water, sanitation, and access to services (health, jobs, education, recreation, and public transportation), housing should provide adequate protection from the elements and security from intruders. It should be secure from the dangers of fire and structural collapse. And finally, it should ensure that residents enjoy adequate space and privacy (Conroy 1987:1).

An opportunity to "operationalize" the various concepts of homelessness came about in 1987, when the United Nations, through the Centre for Human Settlement (Habitat), organized the International Year of Shelter for the Homeless. Habitat received summaries of research reports from 144 countries on the problems of and solutions to homelessness. The final report, *Shelter: From Projects to National Strategies* (United Nations Centre for Human Settlement 1990), is an extremely informative work and includes addresses of governmental and nongovernmental agencies active throughout the world.

The U.N. study concluded that an estimated one billion people either live under conditions of inadequate shelter or are literally homeless. The majority of these people live in the developing countries of the world. It is estimated that as many as 40 to 50 percent of the inhabitants of some of the cities of the developing world live in slums and informal settlements, the result of high rates of population growth and urbanization, large-scale underemployment, and high levels of external debt (United Nations Centre for Human Settlements 1990). In the majority of cases, these people live within families.

In the industrialized countries, the U.N. study concluded that although public agencies have a long tradition of housing construction for the low-income sector, major shelter problems for the poor exist in terms of the maintenance, rehabilitation, or replacement of the existing number of dwellings and in support for special groups such as the single-parent household, the aged, and the handicapped. In the countries of Eastern Europe, where the right to adequate housing has been universal and where governments have assumed almost full responsibility for its provision, no one is "literally" homeless, but the existing housing stock is insufficient and families must often share such facilities as bathrooms and kitchens. As we shall see later in this book, many Western countries have witnessed a decrease in government spending on public housing, as well as a loss of affordable rental housing, through its conversion to upper-income housing or to commercial property. In addition, some Eastern European countries have begun to neglect their guarantee of housing.

Linguistic Clues to Concepts of Homelessness

The words used for the homeless in different cultures give us a clue as to how they are viewed within each culture (see Table 1.1).

For example, the British "sleeping in the rough," the Indian "roofless," the French *sans-abri* (without shade), and the Spanish *sin techos* (roofless) are all descriptive of sleeping outside, without implying either negative personal characteristics or lack of family relationships. On the other hand, terms such as the Spanish *desamparado* (without protection or comfort from other people), the Japanese *furosha* (floating people), the Finnish *puliukko* (elderly male alcoholic), or the American/English "homeless" imply the loss of family and social relationships. These words more clearly conform to the classic "detachment" definition of homelessness.

TABLE 1.1

Conceptualizations of Homelessness in International Perspective

Lack of shelter

roofless (India)

sin techo (Latin America)

sans-abri (France, Canada)

sleeping rough (United Kingdom)

without permanent address (generic term in many languages)

Cut off from a household or other people

homeless

clochard (tramp, France)

pennebruder (men who share sleeping quarters; prison brothers, Germany)

desamparado (without protection or comfort from other people, Latin America)

furosha (floating people, Japan)

tuna wisma, orang gelandangan (uneducated, poor, suspected of crime, Indonesia)

puliukko (elderly male alcoholic who sleeps under bridges, Finland)

Homeless, street children

gamino/a (Colombia)

pivete or pixote (street child involved in crime; pixote is from the movie *Pixote*, Brazil)

khate (rag picker, Kathmandu, Nepal)

parking boy (from common job in informal economy, Nairobi, Kenya)

Squatter settlements, spontaneous settlements

bidonvilles (tin cities, Francophone Africa, France)

pueblos jóvenes (young towns, Lima, Peru)

mong liu, nong min gong (former peasants who move into the city illegally, and sleep in railroad stations, harbors, and in empty buildings/China)

favelas (Brazil)

squats (England)

kampung (Indonesia)

Commonly linked associations with homelessness

rural-to-urban migration

chronic alcoholism

lack of affordable housing due to gentrification, discontinuation of government support for social housing, poor economy

deinstitutionalization of the mentally ill

Some terms evoke historical and literary images, such as hobo, tramp, vagrant, and *clochard* (tramp in French). In some countries special words exist for children on the street such as *gaminos* for the street children of Bogotá, Colombia, *khate* (rag pickers) for those of Kathmandu, Nepal (Child Workers in Nepal Concerned Center 1990), and "parking boys" for those of Nairobi, Kenya (Schenk 1991).

When we expand the concept of homelessness to include those marginally and precariously housed, we find an extensive literature on squatter (also termed spontaneous or informal) settlements, most of which are found in developing countries. Squatter settlements are typically places where people are illegally living on land that they have taken over ("invaded") and on which they have built a shelter out of scavenged material including cardboard, tin, mud, plastic, dung, and rubber tires. These settlements may be known as *favelas* (Brazil), *bidonvilles* (francophone Africa), *pueblos jóvenes* (Peru), *bustees* (India), *gecekondus* (Turkey), *katchi abadis* (Pakistan), *squats* (England), or "homesteading abandoned apartment buildings" (United States). These words are not synonymous, and imply various ways of viewing the settlements. For example, *bidonvilles* (tin cities) has a very different connotation than *pueblos jóvenes* (young towns).

In addition to knowing the strict definitions of the words used for homelessness, it is also important to understand their popular meanings and connotations. For example, to English speakers the word "gamine," similar to the Spanish *gamino/a* (and both related to the French *gamin*), might imply an impish, cute young person. However, as we shall see in the chapter on homeless children, *gamino/a* takes on quite a different connotation in the Latin American context in which the term is employed.

Types of Research on Homelessness

There are several types of research on homelessness. One is quantification—counting the numbers of homeless people. Many research studies try to assess systematically the dimension of homelessness within an area. This is always complicated, because those who are visible on the street and appear homeless may not be homeless, and those who blend into the nonhomeless population may indeed be homeless. Counting the homeless is a key task, since often such an enumeration dictates the level of effort expended to help the homeless. Some countries, like the United States and India, have tried to enumerate the homeless systematically as a part of their nationwide census. Issues of enumeration are discussed in chapter six.

Closely tied to quantification is the task of defining homelessness operationally. Most often there is a several-tiered approach to defining homelessness, from those who sleep outside, to those in shelters and reception areas specifically set up for the homeless, to people sleeping in conditions so bad as to endanger their health, safety, and even survival.

Another type of research is the case-study method. Here, the researcher comes to know an individual, family, or group of people who are homeless, usually through some combination of participant observation and interviews, and describes their situation. For many readers, these reports "bring to life" the homeless situation. Such studies as the book *Rachel and Her Children* (Kozol 1988) and the television accounts of the street children of Rio de Janeiro being murdered during the night (Brokaw 1991) can galvanize the public's attention, at least momentarily.

A topic of considerable study has been projects to upgrade squatter settlements. Projects seek to bring services to squatter communities, usually beginning with potable water and sanitation, and to enable people to gain legal claim to their dwelling and land. Proponents of the upgrading projects (see Turner 1976) point out that these projects reinforce the creativity and self-determination of the people most affected by strengthening housing that already exists, rather than erecting developments that may not be culturally congruent with those living in them. Critics of the projects point to the very minimal standards of the housing, and feel that these projects may absolve governments from more costly but higher quality solutions to the housing issue.

There has been much research on slums, which are generally understood to be old and deteriorated housing within cities. In 1980, the United Nations sponsored a study of slums, with case studies from seven cities in Sri Lanka, the Philippines, Indonesia, Thailand, and India (Sarin 1980).

Beyond the research on housing and homelessness is a substantial body of knowledge concerning the growth of urbanization in the Third World and the consequent increase in the lack of housing for much of the population (see Gugler 1988; Cole 1987; Drakakis-Smith 1987; and Dogan and Kasarda 1988).

In addition to the work of the United Nations, there have been several other broad efforts to synthesize our knowledge of homelessness. Most authors address themselves to homelessness in either the industrialized world (see Friedrichs 1988) or the Third World (see Turner 1976; Payne 1989; Ward 1982; Hardoy and Satterthwaite 1981, 1989; and Murison and Lea 1979). The important work of McAuslan (1985) analyzes causes of homelessness in both industrialized and Third World countries.

The emphasis of much of the world literature on homelessness is devoted to describing informal housing and to suggesting improved methods of construction. Fewer studies concentrate on presenting the difficult lives of homeless people, although anthropologists and some qualitative sociologists have undertaken ethnographic studies to understand their plight. This labor-intensive ethnographic work can be very valuable. For example, the work of Baxter and Hopper (1981) on the streets and subways of New York City was used as court evidence to improve the city's shelter system.

In choosing from the body of research on homelessness, I have selected those studies and reports that contain explicit descriptions of the methodology used. Too often in the field of homelessness, numbers are cited, causes postulated, and conclusions drawn based on unexplained research. This is to some degree understandable because the topic of homelessness arouses a strong emotional response from many people. Homelessness makes poverty visible and concrete. It also represents an affront to our collective sense of what should be a person's right to a minimum standard of existence. Homelessness makes clear how societies fail their most vulnerable members. Nevertheless, I had to set aside books, articles, and reports that were vague in terms of data and methodology.

Causes of Homelessness

Two perspectives underlie our thinking about homelessness in a global sense. In the industrialized world, homelessness is explained in terms of a lack of affordable housing (often caused by the discontinuation of government involvement in the building or subsidization of low-cost housing and the gentrification of the cities) *coupled* with family disintegration, drug and alcohol abuse, and the deinstitutionalization of the

Homeless woman.

Photo by Sandy Hale. Used with permission.

chronically mentally ill, all of which leads to a homeless population on the streets and in the shelters. In the developing world, on the other hand, the explanation centers on issues of rural to urban migration, severe unemployment and underemployment (at least due in part to a colonial history that reduced traditional modes of survival), the existence of large numbers of refugees, and the presence of victims of disasters. Homelessness in the developing world has led to the formation of self-made housing in and near the cities and a growing population of children living on the street. Significantly, the term homelessness is most often associated with industrialized and Western nations.

Lifeways Outside the Purview of This Book

Nomadic people are those whose culture includes having "no fixed address" and moving from place to place. They fall outside of most discussions of homelessness. Examples of nomadic people include pastoralists who move with their herds and have no permanent settlement, such as the Kurds of Iraq (Nanda 1991); hunters and gatherers, such as the !Kung of the Kalahari desert (Shostak 1983); and the Gypsies (known as Travellers throughout the United Kingdom), who move depending on their source of livelihood.

At times, this demarkation between nomadic and homeless people can become blurred. The British anthropologist Judith Okely (1983), for example, has hypothesized that the early Gypsies in England were, in large part, composed of indigenous wanderers. According to her, by the middle of the sixteenth century, vagrants were claiming to be "Egyptians" (later shortened to Gypsies) in order to capitalize on and exploit an exotic identity to gain earnings as fortune-tellers and dancers. At times, those adopting the self-ascription of Egyptian even blackened their faces to substantiate the claim. An interesting contemporary example of wanderers adopting an appellation that suggests a cultural niche is the New Age Travellers of Wales, groups of young people who travel around the United Kingdom in caravans or move into squats (abandoned buildings). They do not consider themselves as homeless, but as having chosen a travel-oriented life-style. They use the name "travellers" (with the modifier "New Age") to characterize this life-style, although the Travellers (Gypsies) do not recognize them as a part of their group (Hutson 1993).

Organization of the Book

Our knowledge of world homelessness, as summarized here, is organized primarily around four categories of people: men, women, children, and families. Within each chapter, I draw attention to the major themes of homelessness within each category, discussing historical perspectives, descriptions (quantitative and qualitative) of homelessness, survival strategies employed by the homeless, health issues, and, finally, the programs and policies that address homelessness. Many categories overlap. For example, homeless children are discussed in relation to both themselves and their families. Moreover, information from one category often applies to another. For example, although tuberculosis among the homeless is discussed in the chapter on men, this same issue applies as well to women.

I have made a concerted attempt to survey as many regions of the world as possible. This in effect means severely limiting the quantity of material on the United States. It also means at times having only one description from a given country (e.g., Denmark), which is less than ideal. As this book represents one of the first attempts to discuss homelessness from a global perspective, I have tried to balance the discussion of the industrialized and developed world. A final chapter on counting the homeless discusses several nationwide and citywide efforts to census their population.

In many ways, there is a numbing sameness when homelessness is looked at in global perspective. Children on the street seek out one another for survival, whether on the streets of Moscow or São Paulo. Poor men without families are relegated to a separate section of the city and quickly forgotten, whether the place is Tokyo or New York. Families move into run-down, heatless apartments from Paris to London to Philadelphia. Hundreds of thousands of people arrive in cities of the developing world, only to build a rudimentary shelter from available material, on land from which they can be removed at any time. Each day, homeless people everywhere risk both their health and their survival.

2

Homeless Men

Naked and shivering, we lined up in the passage. You cannot conceive what ruinous, degenerate curs we looked, standing there in the merciless morning light. A tramp's clothes are bad, but they conceal far worse things; to see him as he really is, unmitigated, you must see him naked. Flat feet, pot bellies, hollow chests, sagging muscles—every kind of physical rottenness was there. Nearly everyone was under-nourished, and some clearly diseased. . . .

The inspection was designed merely to detect smallpox, and took no notice of our general condition. A young medical student, smoking a cigarette, walked rapidly along the line glancing us up and down, and not inquiring whether any man was well or ill. When my cell companion stripped I saw that his chest was covered with a red rash, and, having spent the night a few inches way from him, I fell into a panic about smallpox. The doctor, however, examined the rash and said that it was due merely to under-nourishment. (Orwell 1933:147–148)

> I been a-havin' some hard travellin',
> I thought you knowed,
> I been a-havin' some hard travellin',
> Way down the road,
> I been a-havin' some hard travellin',
> Hard ramblin', hard gamblin',
> I been havin' some hard travellin'.
> (Woody Guthrie 1959)

13

Room for Two, circa 1940.

Photograph by John Albok. Museum of the City of New York, 38.433.38. Gift of the Artist.

Until very recently, homelessness meant homeless men, portrayed as sick and lonely creatures, as in the Orwell quote, or as the fiercely independent "travelling man" immortalized by folksinger and composer Woody Guthrie. A third image, of the saintly mendicant who has renounced all worldly goods and attachments, also exists. In some discussions, there is a sense of fear and danger attached to the homeless man who has cast off societal expectations and norms—who, for many, represents a menace to society.

Words used to define the homeless man such as tramp, bum, *clochard* (French, tramp), *vago* (Spanish, implying laziness), *pennebruder*

(German, negative connotation of men who must share sleeping quarters or who are prison brothers) reflect the disdain with which he is often viewed. In Indonesian the word *gelandangan* means "those who run about" (Ng 1991) and also implies "uneducated, poor, and suspected of becoming involved in criminal activity" (Sjamsir 1991).

In one classic taxonomy, homeless men are categorized by the degree to which they have lost both their affiliation to others and their attachment to work (Caplow, Bahr, and Sternberg 1968:494). The taxonomy consists of single men in itinerant occupations (e.g., peddlers and sailors); migratory laborers; vagrants and beggars; religious mendicants; outlaws and other fugitives; and hoboes and derelicts. A limitation of this typology, however, is that "lack of affiliation" may constitute an ethnocentric view of the (almost always) middle-class observer, who may ignore the social networking in, for example, a soup kitchen (Glasser 1988), or on the streets (Baxter and Hopper 1981).

Historical Perspectives

Historical references to homeless men most often relate to wandering and begging (Gillin 1929; Gilmore 1940; and Cohen and Sokolovsky 1989). Gillin hypothesizes that early human societies did not have beggars and that, as long as men lived in kin-based groups, the nearest analogue to begging was the hospitality asked for by travelers away from home. It is interesting to note that in Finnish, the word for stranger (*vieras*) is the same as the word for guest, implying that, historically, strangers in Finland were taken in as guests (Salo 1988). According to Gillin, the first signs of begging in Western history appear in the eighth century BCE, when beggars begin to be mentioned in the Bible. The arrival of begging coincides with growing commercial activity, and the disruption of the pastoral and agricultural economy.

Throughout history, attitudes toward the wandering beggar have vacillated between tolerance and repression. In the early Christian churches charity was linked with the forgiveness of sin, and almsgiving was viewed as a method of washing away one's sins. As a result, the beggar himself came to represent a sanctified being (Gillin 1929:425).

Early wanderers also functioned as entertainment and as a link to the outside world: "the vagabonds of medieval England and Europe kept jokes, stories, tricks, and news of afar to prolong their welcome. Indeed, the arrival of any stranger probably broke up the monotony of life in the feudal manor (Cohen and Sokolovsky 1989:41).

By the middle of the fourteenth century, numerous economic and social disturbances, including the Black Plague, wars, the break-up of the feudal manors, and the seeds of the Industrial Revolution of the eighteenth century, dislocated people from their jobs and homes, sending them to the streets to beg. As a societal reaction to these people, increasingly severe laws were implemented against "sturdy beggars," meaning those able to work.

> [A]ny vagabond may be taken up by anyone who has offered him work and been refused, brought before two justices, who were to mark him with a hot iron on the breast with the letter V (vagabond) and hand him over to the person presenting him as a slave for two years. If he ran away, he was to be branded on the forehead or ball of the cheek with the letter S. If he ran away a second time, he was to suffer death as a felon. (Gillin 1929:427)

As death rates declined in England and continental Europe and the population grew, an even greater number of people could be found wandering and begging (Piven and Cloward 1971). Governments reacted to the turmoil created by wandering bands of homeless people by introducing relief programs. Over a four-hundred-year history of welfare in England, Western Europe, and the United States, the general pattern has been that relief laws are tied to labor fluctuations. In times of great unemployment and outbreaks of turmoil, relief programs serve to restore order; in times of relative calm, relief systems contract, in order to provide needed workers for the labor market (Piven and Cloward 1971:3). A corollary to this pattern is that severe punishments must be demanded of those who refuse to work. By 1603 the Elizabethan Poor Laws provided that the able-bodied vagrant be sent to the workhouse (termed "indoor relief") and, if he refused, be imprisoned, banished, or executed. The impotent poor (i.e., the disabled) were permitted to beg and often were given a license.

In the United States, the greatest proportion of homeless in the nineteenth century were sailors (Wallace 1965, as cited in Cohen and Sokolovsky 1989). The first shelter in New York City is thought to have been the Sailors' Snug Harbor, established in 1833. Eventually, in both

Europe and the United States, the almshouse, workhouse, and labor colonies led to the establishment of differentiated institutions (asylums) for the physically and mentally disabled. In the latter part of the twentieth century, these institutions, which had become large, depersonalized places, lost favor, and a period of deinstitutionalization led many back to the streets.

The Hobo and Skid Row

Among the studies on homeless men, there is a substantial body of research focusing on the United States from the start of the twentieth century to the present that might be called hobo and skid row literature. Such research likely was inspired by the same factor that led to books and songs about the hobo: the perception of him as the embodiment of the independent, frontier man. Although most people did not dare to take to the road themselves, they often maintained a quiet admiration for the man who did.

In an early and now classic ethnographic study of homeless men, Nels Anderson lived among a community of them in Chicago for twelve months, collecting sixty life histories. His book *The Hobo* (1923) has become a classic and a model of participant observation research.

An entire genre of hobo songs and ballads has been created, often not by homeless men themselves, but by people who knew enough about life on the road to capture its spirit. Some of the best poems were written in prison. In addition to the hymns to the "wanderlust" and songs of political protest against low-wage work, there exists a number of songs that describe the emptiness of religion as a source of relief.

> Long haired preachers come out every night,
> Try to tell you what's wrong and what's right;
> But when asked how 'bout something to eat
> They will answer in voices so sweet;
>
> Chorus
>
> You will eat bye and bye
> In that glorious land above the sky
> Work and pray, live on hay,
> You'll get pie in the sky when you die.
> (Anderson 1923:210)

Skid rows became prevalent in American cities at the close of the Civil War, as thousands of people were uprooted from their homes (Wallace 1965). A contributing factor to the rise of skid rows was the economic panic of 1873 (Black September), during which 30 percent to 40 percent of the population became unemployed. Before the panic, homeless people had slept wherever they could, but now, as neighborhoods became filled with homeless men, this was no longer a viable option. Out of sheer necessity, they were forced to find refuge together in older, run-down parts of town, which came to be known as skid rows.

The term skid row originated from a place in Seattle, Washington, called Skid Road, a trail down which logs were skidded to sawmills, amid a concentration of cheap housing in which the lumberjacks lived (Cohen and Sokolovsky 1989:50). Although the term "homeless" appears to predate any reference to skid rows, it came to mean the people on skid row who either were not working or were migrant or casual laborers between jobs. The skid row inhabitant appears to have acquired the label "homeless" as a result of three factors: his not working while living on skid row, his not having much family contact, and his traveling life-style.

Descriptions of Homeless Men

There is contemporary documentation from England, Italy, France, Japan, the United States, Denmark, and Hong Kong that describes homeless men on the street, in shelters, and on skid row.

The Street

Today, there is a growing presence of homeless people on the streets of the world's cities. For example, in London:

> Just before midnight, an unmarked Salvation Army van pulled up to the curb outside Euston Station and a trickle of tattered men and women edged cautiously from the shadows around the railroad terminal, hunched against the biting winter air.
>
> There were, in all, about 30 of them, many wrapped in blankets. Most were young, in their early 20's, a few smelling sharply of alcohol. (Schmidt 1992:1)

Similar patterns exist in Paris, Amsterdam, Madrid, and Rome, as well as in the smaller cities of Western Europe. The problem is due to myriad factors: a reduction in the number of units of low-cost rental housing, the loss of jobs and income as the global economy worsens, deterioration of the network of family, church, and governmental support, and, in Britain and Italy, as well as in North America, the deinstitutionalization of the mentally ill.

> "It is a bad sign indicating the strength of the Italian family is beginning to wane," said Francesca Zuccari, a volunteer worker who wrote a booklet for the homeless in Italy titled "Where to Eat, to Sleep, to Wash," distributed from the St. Egidio Community Center in Trastevere. (Schmidt 1992:8)

In Paris, much of the problem of homelessness may be due to high rents and a 10 percent unemployment rate:

> A beggar hops into a Paris subway car as the doors slam and begins his familiar litany:
> "Ladies and gentlemen, thank you for listening. I am 30 years old, unemployed and homeless. I have a wife and two children. I haven't fed them for three days."
> An elegantly coiffed woman in a tweed suit wrinkles her nose and turns away. Farther down the car, two businessmen discreetly bury themselves in their copies of *Le Monde*.
> The beggar is disheveled and unshaven, his thick gray socks torn and black with dirt. He has no shoes. Slowly he moves round the car asking for money.
> "Thank you, thank you," he says as a few coins drop into his hand.
> (Gumpel 1992:7A)

Although African immigrants are considered a minority of the estimated 15,000 to 20,000 homeless in Paris, they are believed to be the most tenuously housed, often living six to eight to a room, with no water or heat. They are also often the focus of the population's anger and are scapegoated for various social ills, including homelessness.

In Japan, men camping out in tunnels are common in Tokyo, Yokohama, and Osaka (Weisman 1991). Many of them appear to suffer from alcoholism and mental illness. They are allowed to stay on the streets unless they disturb someone. The homeless appear to include a sizable proportion of Koreans (an ethnic minority in Japan) and Burakumin, an untouchable-like lower caste:

> In a silent, dark alley near piers that bustle during the day, a few small piles of cardboard and blankets are all that keep the late-night chill from 10 sleeping men, a handful of the scores of homeless vagrants of this otherwise prosperous port.
>
> "I chose this way of life myself no one chose it for me," said Yuji Inoue, a grizzled 64-year-old unemployed construction worker, stirring momentarily for a cigarette and some conversation. "The people who come by and see me, well, no one is hostile. But nobody's giving me money either." (Weisman 1991:4)

For the most part, these homeless men are comprised of workers who reside in flophouses (when not literally homeless) in places such as Kotobukicho, a once prosperous (pre–World War II) district of Yokohama that was rebuilt after the war as a site for cheap hotels housing laborers working in construction and at the American navy base. Kotobukicho is an example of a day laborers' community, called a *yoseba* in Japanese, where as many as 10,000 men live and seek day work (see Hester 1991 for an excellent discussion of day laborers' communities of Japan). The peak times of Japanese homelessness occur during the New Year's period when construction shuts down.

There are groups of volunteers who offer the homeless blankets and encourage them to sign up for help: "'We are careful not to become too familiar with the people we help because it's a shameful thing for them,' said Yoh Nonomura, a volunteer. 'They get annoyed even if we ask them their names. They generally want to be left alone'" (Weisman 1991:4).

In Japan a common word for the homeless is *furosha*, which literally means floating person, but is also synonymous with tramp and wanderer (Ohya 1992; Hester 1993). It is interesting to note in reference to explanations for homelessness that in contrast to the United States and England, Japan has *not* emptied its mental hospitals during the last twenty years, and that there are now twice as many mental patients as there were twenty-five years ago, many of whom would have been on the street otherwise. It is also interesting to note that the homeless of Japan include fewer families or drug addicts than in other industrialized nations.

Shelters

Taking refuge in a shelter is necessary for survival, especially during the cold winters of the northern hemisphere. A firsthand approach to understanding the homeless was taken by John R. Coleman, president of the Edna McConnell Clark Foundation, who posed as a homeless man for ten days in New York City (Coleman 1986). In addition to experiencing the very negative reactions of his fellow citizens and what 12°F really means on the streets at 6 A.M., Coleman discovered the horrors and humiliations of the shelter system.

> At 3:30 p.m., with more cold ahead, I sought out the Men's Shelter at 8 East 3rd Street. This is the principal entry point for men seeking the city's help. It provides meals for 1,300 or so people every day and beds for some few of those. . . .
>
> I've seen plenty of drawings of London's workhouses and asylums in the times of Charles Dickens. Now I've seen the real thing in the last years of the twentieth century in the world's greatest city. . . .
>
> The air was heavy with the odors of Thunderbird wine, urine, sweat and, above all, nicotine and marijuana. Three or four Human Resources Administration police officers seemed to be keeping the violence down to tolerable levels, but barely so. . . .
>
> It was time to get in line to eat. This meant crowding into what I can only compare to a cattle chute in a stockyard. It ran along two walls of the sitting room and was already jammed. A man with a bullhorn kept yelling at us to stand up and stay in line. One very old and decrepit (or drunk?) man couldn't stay on his feet. He was helped to a chair, from which he promptly fell onto the floor. The bullhorn man had some choice obscenities for him, but they didn't seem to have any effect. The old man just lay there, and we turned our thoughts back to the evening meal. (Coleman 1986:44–45)

This situation is not atypical. The Fort Washington Avenue Armory Shelter, also in New York City, contains 933 cots and is an example of the dangers of throwing homeless men into an understaffed cavernous space: "Drug use is rampant, bone-crushing beatings are commonplace, and at night rats scurry across the floor and onto the tightly packed cots" (Gonzalez 1992:B1).

In Denmark, where there are sixteen shelters, problems exist in terms of the provision of services (Langergaard 1992). The Danish Parliament recently passed a law requiring that municipalities and counties share the costs of shelter for the homeless, in contrast to the former situation in which the state assumed 75 percent of the costs. The problem is that many of the homeless are registered in more than one municipality, and each municipality tries to relinquish responsibility for individual persons.

> Many of the clients [i.e., the homeless in shelters] are repeats, and one month they show up at Vibohoj and two months later they are at the shelter in Alborg.

> "They have all of Denmark as their address," says Kjeld Rasmussen [a shelter manager] about the situation of the homeless, when they move away from the streets and seek help at a shelter.

> "These people have no permanent address, and when they leave us, it is almost as if they throw the cap up in the air and walk in the direction it points." (Langergaard 1992: 2–3)

If the municipalities refuse to support the shelters, the government of Denmark may have to take responsibility for the *papkassefolk* (cardboard box people) itself, which will mean a new challenge for a country with a long tradition of social responsibility.

Skid Row

Skid rows are places of inexpensive lodging, usually within large cities, that house men who either don't work or work sporadically. These areas of the city, considered a blight by the more affluent, in fact serve as a refuge for the man who is alone in life.

There is an excellent body of ethnographic literature that describes in detail the day-to-day life and survival of men on skid row. Jacqueline Wiseman (1970) and James Spradley (1970) concentrate on the adaptation for survival of alcoholic men on skid row. One of their findings is that a great *heterogeneity* exists among the homeless men there. David Levinson (1974), in an ethnographic study of men in New York's

Bowery, in addition to describing survival strategies, notes an increase in both crime and the number of younger men. He quotes one Bowery resident as saying, "Fifteen years ago I could sit down here [on the sidewalk], lean back, and go to sleep with fifty dollars in my pocket and no one would bother me. Now I get hit over the head for a dime. It's no good, too rough" (Levinson 1974:26). Writing ten years after the publication of her 1970 book, *Stations of the Lost*, Wiseman noted an increase in younger people, blacks and hispanics, females, and former flower children, whom she calls "Woodstock Nation in tatters" (Wiseman 1970:xiii).

Cohen and Sokolovsky (1989) introduce the reader to three Bowery men, each of whom represents a different type of homeless person. Uncle Ed is an alcoholic with a long history on the Bowery. Miles is a working man whose life began to fall apart at the age of fifty. Finally, Roland, a man with psychiatric disabilities, has found a niche

The Bowery, circa 1935.

Photograph by Reginald Marsh. Museum of the City of New York.

for himself on the Bowery helping out the social service institutions of the area.

Uncle Ed, the Classic Bowery Man:

Uncle Ed is a jovial caricature of the classic skid row alcoholic. Nicknamed by a nurse because of his helpful and affable attitude toward others while he was a patient at a "sobering up station," he tried to show a non offensive helpful tact to all he meets. A comely clean-shaven person when sober, he is usually dressed in second-hand mission clothes that tend to be misfitted to his bulky frame and pot belly. (Cohen and Sokolovsky 1989:2)

Miles, the Fry Cook:

It is now a summer day. Miles rises before daybreak from his park bench at East 23rd Street. Despite his tall lean frame and healthy looks, old age hangs on this black man's shoulders like a leaden cloak. At first light he begins what for him is a humiliating task, collecting returnable soda and beer cans. . . .

Miles's life had not always been this way. After World War II he began working as a cook's helper at a seafood restaurant that attracted hundreds of patrons. . . . It was two decades later that his life began to come apart. In 1972, at the age of 50, he had the first of several heart attacks, and shortly after he was released from the hospital, the restaurant closed. Without his old job, and in poor health, he began a pattern of periodic drinking. . . . (Cohen and Sokolovsky 1989:5–6)

Roland, the Super-Runner:

"Not even the cops will bother me here," Roland said confidently as he closed the top of his room for the night—a cardboard carton which last housed a new refrigerator. As a final ritual to evoke momentary security he pulled his woolen cap over his gaunt, well-scrubbed cheeks and curled up into a ball.

Roland is a "do-gooder" who labors for the charity establishment rather than the tavern owners or hotel managers because he has acquired the social work ethic. Each weekday at noon he becomes the delivery unit of the Bowery's main "meals on wheels" program. Up and down the steps of flophouses he can be seen effortlessly hefting a cart laden with prepared lunches from a local soup kitchen. (Cohen and Sokolovsky 1989:9–10)

The heterogeneity noted in the skid rows of the United States is also found in Winnipeg, Canada. In an eight-year study (1976 to 1984), Christopher Hauch discovered that the largest group on Winnipeg's skid row was made up of Canadian Indians, who spent time on skid row and then went back to the reserves or to seasonal jobs (1985). The rest of the men also spent only intermittent time on skid row, leaving to go to work. Interestingly, Hauch found that, when the news media came to write an exposé about Winnipeg's skid row, they found few longtime residents living there. Nevertheless, these were labeled "typical," thereby giving a distorted view of the area. Hauch critiques the media's penchant for spotlighting only the most populated and public places and not portraying the tedium of life on skid row. In one instance, he observed reporters lying on the ground, posing for each other, because they could not find a cooperative resident for their story.

The "cage" apartments in Hong Kong are another type of skid row accommodation for homeless men. The cages, which resemble those in a zoo and measure 6 feet long, 30 inches wide, and 30 inches tall, are stacked three high and rent for an average of $150 a month. "'The top cage is cheapest,' said Mr. Cho, a 57-year-old living up top. 'It's the hardest to climb into. The bottom is second cheapest—you're easily disturbed. The middle level is the expensive one'" (Terrill 1991:112).

Cage apartments house the elderly, sick, and disabled; it is estimated that 5,000 people sleep this way. At 26 Fuk Tsun Street in Hong Kong, the cages hold all of the men's belongings, in addition to serving as their bed at night. "All around us, men in shorts watched cartoons on a communal television and played cards or chess as Chinese opera blared from a radio. Mr. Kwan, the superintendent of the place, said fights are rare, despite the crowded conditions" (Terrill 1991:112).

Survival Strategies

One of the most frequent modes of survival for a homeless person is begging, although not all beggars are homeless. Begging is one of the many "street occupations," which include retail distribution (such as selling foodstuffs), personal services (such as shoeshining), recuperation (door-to-door collection of old newspapers), and prostitution (Bromley 1988). Some experts urge that begging be referred to as "work" because it is activity "where time and effort are expended in the pursuit of monetary gain or of material gain derived from other persons in exchange for the worker's labour or products of such labour" (Bromley 1988:165). However, begging and other street occupations are generally not considered work by nonstreet people.

As was true in an earlier era, contemporary begging still appears to be related to concepts of religion. For example, in a study (1971) of eighty-seven beggars in San Cristóbal de las Casas, a city of 25,000 people in the southeastern state of Chiapas, Mexico, Horacio Fabrega, a psychiatrist and anthropologist, found the city's beggars to be primarily men who had lived in the surrounding villages, who suffered a medical disability, and were poor and alone in life. They had migrated to the city, which is known for its long-standing religious tradition, in order to survive by what Fabrega terms "the informal welfare system of begging." (In a similar fashion, elderly people in Taiwan are reported to flock to the Wanhua region of Taipei because of the great number of temples and sanctuaries there [Boehi 1991].)

Beggars in San Cristóbal are called *limosneros*, derived from the word *limosna*, meaning alms. The *limosneros* are generally thought of in one of two categories: those with an obvious physical deformity who appear unable to work and those with no visible deformity. The male *limosnero* is most often barefoot and unshaven, and typically walks in a crouch. A request for alms usually is made by appealing to religious feelings, by asking for *"un limosnito, un favorcito"* (diminutive form of alms, favor). A *limosnero* with an obvious deformity need only sit with a plate for the offerings next to him.

Fabrega made initial contact with the beggars on the street, and then interviewed them at several local homes. In addition to collecting life histories of many of the beggars, he was able to do a physical exam to determine their health status. Almost 60 percent of the overall group had a visible physical deformity, mostly caused by a traumatic accident, or a handicap such as blindness. (Fabrega suggests that the cause of blindness in these men is onchocerciasis, endemic in the coffee plantations where many of them had worked.)

Most of the beggars in Fabrega's study "borrowed" the corridor or patio of someone's house as a place to sleep, although some slept on the streets. Even in the borrowed places, they were usually not allowed to use the toilet.

About two-thirds of the *limosneros* begged in San Cristóbal exclusively, although the Indians of the group who were still attached to a household in the surrounding countryside would return there every two or three weeks. Another third of the beggars were "itinerant beggars," traveling to nearby cities and to Guatemala to beg. Very few beggars in the study were permanently housed.

Whereas the beggars of San Cristóbal flock to the city because of its reputation for charity, the ascetics of India take to the road in order to spend the last years of their life seeking spiritual perfection (Tyler 1973). Some modern Indian intellectuals believe that the ascetic is a social parasite who makes no contribution to society. Others (and Tyler maintains them to be the great majority of Indian people) feel that he is the embodiment of India's spiritualism and a living deity.

Another religious tradition that includes traveling from place to place and begging is the network of Koranic schools of Muslim society in Western Africa (Lubeck 1981). Rural children are sent to a *mallam* (teacher) to study the Koran, increase skills for work (for example, to learn the indigo dyeing industry), and to lessen the risk of famine for the rural household. Begging through the Koranic schools may be seen as a form of redistribution of wealth from the more affluent urban dwellers to the sons of rural dwellers under the norms of Islamic charity (Lubeck 1981). As an indication of the acceptance of begging done by the Koranic scholars, some factory workers reported that in their youth they had posed as Koranic students in order to receive the alms distributed in the evening to the students who chanted Koranic verses for households (Lubeck 1981:72).

A general observation about men on the streets is that they have a cyclical sense of time rather than the linear sense of time, characteristic of the rest of society, with its concern for the past and future (Murray 1986). Because the homeless man is so dependent on the people and institutions that help him survive, he focuses on their daily and monthly cycles—the time the soup kitchen opens, the time the shelter closes its doors, or the day the welfare check comes. Rather than reflecting an inability to plan for the future, this cyclical sense of time is adaptive for the homeless man surviving on the streets.

Health Issues

Life as a homeless person can have severe consequences in terms of health. The exposure to the elements, poor diet, sleep deprivation, risk of violence, injuries, and little or no health care lead to a precarious state of health and exacerbate any preexisting illnesses. Three health conditions that are closely associated with homeless men are alcoholism, mental illness, and tuberculosis.

Alcoholism

No health condition is more closely tied to homelessness in the popular mind than alcoholism. References to "smelling of alcohol" and "thought to be alcoholic" abound in the world literature on homelessness. However, there appear to be few actual research studies that have tried to address this issue systematically. Given the variable definitions of alcohol abuse and of homelessness, it is a subject that is complicated when addressed in global perspective.

Much of what we reliably know about the health of the homeless comes from the work of Wright and Weber (1987), who conducted the Health Care for the Homeless Program, which established health clinics in nineteen U.S. cities for four years and was funded for $25 million by the Robert Wood Johnson Foundation and the Pew Memorial Trust. In addition to standard physical health care, these clinics included services for mental health, dental care, podiatry, alcoholism rehabilitation, an extensive system of referral to other health and social service facilities, and respite care (for recently discharged homeless hospital patients). After one year of operation, the clinics had seen 34,035 individuals an average of 2.7 times. One conclusion of the project was that continuous health care could be provided for the most marginal segment of the urban poor through this type of health care program.

In the past the incidence of alcohol abuse among the homeless was higher, and was considered the primary cause of homelessness. Currently, alcohol abuse afflicts an estimated two-fifths of the U.S. homeless population. The combined effects of alcoholism and homelessness include a wide array of neurological, circulatory, endocrinological, and digestive disorders, as well as infectious diseases. In the Health Care for the Homeless Program, the alcohol abuser appeared to be at greater risk for neurological impairment, heart disease and hypertension, chronic lung disease, gastrointestinal disorders, hepatic dysfunction, and trauma, in comparison to the rest of the homeless patients seen by the clinics (Wright and Weber 1987:69). An interesting finding of this study is that the rate of alcohol abuse among homeless men appeared to be three times the rate of alcohol abuse among homeless women. The highest rates of alcohol abuse among both men and women were among the Native Americans, and the lowest rates among Hispanics and Asians.

An example of a homeless alcoholic in the United States known by the Health Care for the Homeless Program is a man named Radar, who had been in and out of detoxification units 480 times, according to his own count. Parts of his life story follow:

> Radar was born in a New England Mill town to a rigid military family. His parents were social drinkers, but neither he nor his sister were allowed to drink or swear. . . . Radar had his first drink on the night of his high school graduation and in a fundamental sense, he has not stopped drinking since. . . .
>
> "You learn how to get along. In the summer you sleep out, mostly in the cemetery. You lay some cardboard down on the ground, cause it gets damp, you know. When you get up, you 'rough up' the grass so nobody knows you been there. Sometimes you find a shiny tombstone and you use it like a mirror, to see yourself. You keep a toothbrush and some aftershave on you. You take the salt from a fast food restaurant to brush your teeth, and splash on some aftershave to cover up, you know. Unless you have to drink it." (Wright and Weber 1987:66)

An indication of how closely tied alcoholism and homelessness are in much of the world is that in Finnish the modern popular words used for homeless people typically have the first meaning of a single male alcoholic living under the bridges of a city (Summa 1991:199). One of the words for homeless, *puliukko* (old alcoholic), is derived from the words "ukko" (old man) and "puli," which comes from the noun "pulituuri," meaning varnish/lacquer (Taipale 1979, as cited in Kylmala 1991).

In the 1980s Finland tried to "delabel" the homeless in order to distance them from the alcoholic image (Summa 1991). The result is a coded language in which the homeless are referred to as those having "certain individual needs and inclinations" (Summa 1991:204).

There is some concern as to whether researchers in the field of homelessness tend to ignore or underestimate the alcoholism of the people they study (Room 1984; Kylmala 1991). This may be because of discomfort with the topic (because they drink themselves?) or because they are not well trained in alcoholism research. Another factor may be that in the interests of advocacy work, discussions of alcoholism, drug use, or mental illness might deflect attention from societal responsibility for housing.

When homelessness is mixed with alcoholism, freezing to death becomes an ever-present risk. The city of Anchorage, Alaska, has several aggressive and apparently successful programs to prevent homeless alcoholics from freezing to death in a city where the average winter low is 7°F (DeParle 1992a). There, the Community Service Patrol scours the city with a van, picking up people who have fallen asleep (apparently from drink) on the sidewalks or in the bushes and are in danger of freezing. These people are then taken to a hospital (if they need to go), to the city's Brother Francis Shelter (which shelters up to 320 per night), or to an emergency "sleep-off" center, which can house thirty people who are too drunk to go to the shelter.

> Saving the lives of street alcoholics is an unassailable goal, but is also ugly work. And no one knows it better than Kirk Roberts, a medical technician who spends his days dragging them from bushes, sidewalks and alleys.
>
> "C'mon, Manny, be cool," he pleaded one August night to a resisting man, who five minutes earlier was lying unconscious in a park.
>
> Now bouncing in the back of an emergency van, the man leaned forward menacingly and unfolded his finger into an obscene gesture. He had a blood alcohol level of .435 milligrams per 100 milliliters, more than four times the legal limit for drunkenness. . . .
>
> "Most people will stop breathing at that point," said Mr. Roberts, who had rescued Manuel seven times in six weeks. (DeParle 1992a:B12)

The city's generosity and initiative in working with the homeless are now being questioned as possibly "enabling" alcoholics to continue drinking. As a result, the thirty-bed emergency sleep-off center has been replaced by a bedless waiting room where alcoholics must sit up in hard chairs throughout the night.

Mental Illness

In the United States and some nations in Western Europe it appears that the image of the homeless person has changed from "drunken" to "crazy" (Fischer and Breakey 1986). As in the case of alcohol abuse, the research on the relationship between mental illness and homelessness is complex, and not plentiful in a global context. Is mental illness (subject to a wide variety of definitions) a cause or a result of home-lessness? Wright and Weber (1987) point out that behaviors such as rummaging through the garbage for food or urinating in public may seem "crazy" but are actually adaptations to life on the street. Similarly, symptoms of anxiety and depression may also be situational reactions to a life with much stress and little hope. Even becoming hospitalized in a psychiatric institution may be part of a conscious attempt to get off the streets for a while (Kalifon 1989).

In the United States, estimates of the incidence of mental illness among the homeless range from 15 to 90 percent (Wright and Weber 1987). The Health Care for the Homeless Program estimated a 33 per-cent incidence of mental illness, with a disproportionally high rate of 50 percent occurring among white middle-aged women. The highest rates were among whites of both genders, and the lowest among Latinos (Wright and Weber 1987:93).

Our knowledge of homelessness and mental illness (or any other condition) may be affected by the environment in which studies of the homeless are conducted. For example, in a study from Edinburgh, Scotland, it was found that in comparing a sample of the homeless from common lodging houses to a sample of the homeless from psychiatric inpatient and outpatient services, the latter had greater prevalence in all psychiatric diagnostic categories (as would be expected) *except for* schizophrenia, which occurred almost twice as frequently among the homeless from the common lodging houses (Priest 1976). An interest-ing explanation for this apparent paradox is that "the quietly bizarre and delusional schizophrenic prefers to withdraw from public attention and thus is less likely to enter a treatment setting than others, such as depressed, manic, antisocial, alcoholic, or personality disordered patients, whose insight is greater, whose suffering is more obvious, or whose behavior is more disruptive" (Fischer and Breakey 1986:17).

A central topic in the United States is the issue of to what degree homelessness has been caused by the era of deinstitutionalization of the chronically mentally ill in the last half of the twentieth century. In the United States the psychiatric inpatient population declined from over 559,000 in 1955 to 132,000 in 1983 (Redick and Witkin 1983). This decrease was due mainly to the release of confined patients into the community and stricter guidelines in admitting new patients for long-term care. The anticipated network of community services for these discharged patients was largely nonexistent or inadequate. The term deinstitutionalization itself refers to the discharging of the previously long-term hospitalized patient, to the brief stays of current psychiatric patients (leading to a "revolving door" of health care), and to policies that make admission to psychiatric hospitals more difficult (Bachrach 1984; Glasser 1988).

A combination of mental illness and drugs can produce disturbing and aggressive behaviors. For example, Larry Hogue, a homeless veteran who had become disabled during military service when a propeller blade struck him in the head, causing frontal lobe damage to his brain, until recently occupied a spot on the upper West Side of New York City for about seven years (Dugger 1992c). He receives $36,000 in benefits a year, much of which was spent on crack and other street drugs. His case exemplifies the extent to which society has to tolerate a dangerous street person:

> Peering from their apartment windows, the residents of West 96 Street have watched Larry Hogue's slow descent into madness. At first he was just another shambling homeless man who muttered to himself, slept barefoot in the snow and ate from the garbage.
>
> But over the years his behavior became more bizarre. He stalked a teacher as she walked her fawn-colored Akita, and threatened to roast and eat the dog. He dragged a ragged chair into a busy intersection, leaned back as if he were reclining in a chaise longue and munched a bagel as cars swerved around him.
>
> He jumped on the hood of a red Jetta and banged on the windshield as a terrified woman tried to pull out of a parking space. He heaved rocks through the vaulted stained glass windows of a landmark church. He knocked a school girl into the street where she was almost struck by an onrushing truck. (Dugger 1992c:A1)

Mr. Hogue was repeatedly incarcerated and hospitalized for his behavior, but was released each time, primarily because, without the street drugs, he was quiet and cooperative. There were no grounds to keep him involuntarily committed to a psychiatric hospital. On the other hand, he clearly terrorized the neighborhood and forced some of its inhabitants to move, or at least to change their day-to-day routines.

In developing countries, vagrancy is often associated with mental disorders (Baasher et al. 1983). The term "vagrant psychotic" is used to refer to people behaving strangely by, for example, walking about naked, dressing incongruously, collecting rubbish, chasing rams and goats, or wandering from town to town (Asuni 1968). A vagrant psychotic in this context is a person who is publicly visible and identifiable as a psychotic, but is neither institutionalized nor receiving regular treatment (Baasher 1983). The person might have gone or been taken to a traditional healer, as in the following case:

> [A] young schizophrenic [was seen] at the healing place of an Ethiopian sheik. His mother, after having been abandoned by her husband, was accompanying him on a desperate crusade already lasting four years, moving in vain from one hospital to another, from one traditional healing center to the next. At times she had to lead him with tied hands at the end of a rope. . . . (Workneh and Giel 1975, as cited in Baasher 1983:29)

In Egypt it appears that vagrant female psychotics are hospitalized at a higher rate than their male counterparts, suggesting a more protective attitude toward females. In one study, the records of vagrant psychotics admitted to the Abbassia Psychiatric Hospital in Cairo, Egypt, in 1978 and 1979 were examined (Baasher et al. 1983). Out of the 2,200 admissions over the two-year period, there were 117 cases of vagrant psychotics, and 64 percent of these were women. Another finding was that 90 percent of the vagrants admitted were referred by the police.

As in the industrialized world, the existence of the vagrant psychotic in the developing world is attributed to a combination of a lack of community treatment *and* the shortage of housing for single people. Throughout Africa there are "contact services" such as night shelters or soup runs that offer on the spot services to the homeless. An observation about the vagrant psychotic in Africa that may be relevant to the industrialized world's debate over deinstitutionalization policies is that he or she appears to at least care about where the next meal is coming from and about general issues of survival, in contrast to the apathetic, slow, and disinterested manner of many of the hospitalized patients (Asuni 1968; Giel et al. 1974).

Tuberculosis

A key health issue in the United States today is the resurgence of tuberculosis, especially the drug-resistant form. This resurgence has been attributed to a complex of factors, including a decrease in resources devoted to the surveillance and control of TB, lack of access to medical care and shorter hospital stays, the coincident emergence of the HIV epidemic, the growth of the number of people living in congregate living situations (including prisons and shelters), and an increase of poverty and homelessness (Gostin 1993). The life of homelessness, with exposure to the elements, poor diet, alcoholism, and other illnesses can lead to a decreased resistance to TB (Institute of Medicine 1988). Also, living in crowded shelters or shared quarters can increase the risk of exposure to the TB bacteria, which are transmitted in the droplets of moisture coughed up by a person with an active case of pulmonary TB. The Health Care for the Homeless Program found the rate of active TB infections to be 500 per 100,000, in contrast to the 19 per 100,000 reported in the urban U.S. population in the mid-1980s (Wright and Weber 1987:108–109).

The rising number of multidrug-resistant cases (MDR) of TB means that the length of treatment increases from approximately six months to eighteen to twenty-four months, and that the cure rate decreases from nearly 100 percent to 60 percent or less (Gostin 1993). This disturbing trend is explained by the rise in the number of TB patients who are not completing treatment. Eventually they become resistant to the medication, become infectious again, and are able to spread a virulent form of drug-resistant TB. It is estimated that 40 percent of New York City's 3,673 TB patients, many of whom are homeless or precariously housed, stop taking their pills prematurely (Navarro 1992:1). In an attempt to ameliorate this public health problem, "pill monitors," who give "directly observed therapy," are employed by the New York City Board of Health. These pill monitors, of whom there are fifty, go to the "community" (it could be a park bench) to observe TB patients swallowing their pills. New York City expected to monitor 500 patients in this manner. A problem with this approach, however, is that while following TB patients around the city might inspire more of them to take their medication, it does not address the issue of homelessness that increases the risk of being "noncompliant" in the first place. A suggestion is that homeless TB patients be assigned a public health case manager or advocate who can assist them in obtaining financial benefits, substance abuse or mental health treatment, and housing (Gostin 1993).

One of the suggestions for improving health care for the homeless has been referred to as the "marketing-oriented" approach. The basic goal of this approach is to target health care specifically for the homeless population. It maintains that outreach programs in skid row areas, and shelters and soup kitchens that are staffed by health care providers who have training in working with the homeless, would in the long run reduce health costs by treating health problems in their early stages (Hill 1991).

Programs and Policies for Homeless Men

The most successful projects that address the needs of the homeless man appear to be those that enable him to have a permanent address and stable living environment, while at the same time respecting his independence and considerable survival strategies. Ways of meeting the needs of the homeless man range from making initial contact with him on the street, to a laissez-faire "street city" concept of self-help housing, to group homes and supported living arrangements for the psychiatrically impaired.

One of the services of the Manhattan Bowery Corporation's Midtown Outreach Program in New York City was to drive around the streets and pick up homeless men who wanted to go to a drop-in center where they could take a shower, get a clean change of clothing, and receive medical help. The drive in the van proved to be therapeutic in and of itself, in that it enabled some of the men, who were strangers, to become concerned and involved with one another's welfare. The van ride interaction became known as the "shower group" by the workers of the program.

> The group members were Jim, a mildly retarded overweight white male in his late thirties, Philip, in his early sixties, a self-detoxified recovering alcoholic with alcohol hallucinosis, and Kevin, a young white paranoid schizophrenic suffering from feelings of persecution. Their initial contact with staff in the van formed the basis for developing relationships and interactions among themselves that in time carried over to relationships independent of the team workers. The men began to show concern for others by asking for individuals who were not at their usual pick-up spots at the specified time. Their concern for others served to remind them of the possibilities they faced themselves. (Martin and Nayowith 1988:84)

Eventually these men moved into a hotel and became the nucleus for mutual support among its residents.

Another trend is to try to move the homeless man out of the anonymous and dangerous conditions of large urban shelters into smaller, more service-oriented accommodations. However, a real problem is communities' negative response to locating smaller, more structured, single-room housing shelters in their neighborhoods. This response has been popularized as the NIMBY (not-in-my-backyard) syndrome.

A concern in discussions about housing homeless men is that any change may produce stress, anxiety, and fear of the unknown in the men, and that this apprehension may be justified. For example, in a project in Chicago, homeless men who had been living in six-by-eight-foot huts with no water, electricity, or heat (these huts had been supplied by the Mad Housers, an Atlanta-based hut construction movement) were offered apartments in public housing. However, many were very reluctant to move because they felt safer in their huts than in the drug- and crime-ridden public housing they were being offered (Terry 1992).

Street City in Toronto is an experiment in a democratically run group-living situation for formerly homeless people. In an old warehouse in the industrial part of town, seventy men and women live in a building with separate bedrooms, although they share bathrooms, kitchens, and living rooms. Residents of Street City pay $350 (Canadian dollars) a month if they are on welfare, or one-quarter of their income if they are working. There are two mayors of Street City, who meet with their fellow residents every three weeks to discuss such issues as living conditions, the operation of the residence, and possible improvements (McCann 1992).

In the typology of housing for the homeless there are three types of shelter: independent, supportive, and care facilities. "Independent" housing is made up of self-contained units in which the resident is responsible for his own upkeep (e.g., cooking and cleaning). "Supportive" housing is for people who cannot live alone and require services because of physical disabilities, mental health problems, and/or alcoholism. "Care facilities" consist of places where medical and personal services are supplied by others on a daily basis (Hulchaniski 1991:13–14). Occasionally, a project can combine all three types of services under one roof. Housing schemes for homeless men usually are located in communities in which they are already familiar and feel a sense of support.

> In Vancouver [Canada], many of the problems associated with homelessness are concentrated in the older downtown and eastside neighbourhoods, where older single men on welfare and the majority of World War II veterans who have chronic illnesses reside in Skid Row hotels and

sleeping rooms when they are not sleeping "under the stars." . . . Although it is considered by many to be a hard and unforgiving place, there is a strong sense of community in the area, and residents consider the local streets to be an extension of their living rooms. It is a milieu which is both home and a neighbourhood. A number of highly innovative initiatives have been designed for the long-term residents of the downtown eastside, providing them with secure, affordable, and quality accommodations enabling them to live with dignity in the area of their choice. (Oberlander and Fallick 1987:18)

An example of housing built with a sense of community is the Veteran's Manor at 310 Alexander Street in Vancouver, administered by the Veteran's Memorial Housing Society. A new five-story building of 134 units, the structure accommodates various levels of independent living ranging from the ground floor, which contains units for people who depend on staff, to the top floor, which contains apartments with a private bath and kitchen. Forty units on the first floor and part of the second contain a sink, bed, and basic furniture. The remaining units range from those with a toilet and sink only, to those with a bath and kitchenette, and finally to apartments containing all amenities. The project costs $4.5 million and is funded by the Canada Mortgage and Housing Corporation, the Veterans Affairs Canada, and the City of Vancouver (Oberlander and Fallick 1987:19). An important part of the philosophy of the project is to encourage improvement, but not to force it. In addition to the housing units, the building design calls for a low-cost public cafeteria for the residents and the surrounding community, known as Club 44, so that the men can interact with the people in the community.

The success of providing permanent housing for the formerly homeless can be considerable. Homes First, a Toronto nonprofit group, finds that many emotionally damaged people can blossom and take charge of their own lives within six months of entering a stable and supportive living environment (Ontario Task Force on Roomers, Boarders and Lodgers 1986a:181).

Homeless men, historically the largest group of homeless people, receive only the most meager responses to their problems. Their independence and the public perception of them as threatening, as alcoholics, and as mentally ill put this group last on the list for help. On the other hand, there are a modest number of projects and philosophies that appear to be successful in moving men from the street to a more stable environment.

3

Homeless Women

Last winter Rebecca Smith, age sixty-one, died in New York City. She froze to death in the home she had constructed for herself inside a cardboard box. She preferred it, she said to any other home. (Stoner 1983:565)

In nearly every city there is somewhere to get free food. In New York this means going to the bread line at St. Francis's at five in the morning. In Boston it might be waiting until five in the evening to go to Rosie's Place for dinner. In San Francisco, at St. Anthony's Dining Hall, men start lining up around ten in the morning for lunch at noon while women and the infirm are able to go to the head of the line. . . . For many of these people the focus of their entire day is finding food.

Helen . . . tries to get to St. Anthony's most mornings. I watch her eat the nourishing but none too appetizing scrambled eggs, creamed vegetables, hot dogs, white bread, mashed potatoes, donuts and the surprisingly good coffee that is served. Helen has been talking about the tiny dots on her arms and neck, the pain she is having behind her ears, and the pain she feels in her hands. . . . When I suggest that she check her mattress for bugs as a possible cause of the red dots, she says, "No that couldn't be it because I'm not staying anywhere." (Rousseau 1981:27)

In contrast to homelessness among men, where the very definition of homelessness often has a male connotation (*clochard*, hobo, tramp), homelessness among single women is characterized by its *invisibility*. There are indications that, at least in the Western world, there are and have been homeless women, yet our knowledge of them is minimal, and only recently has sustained attention been given this group. One reason for this may be the tendency for homeless women to stay far from view because of the physical danger of being a woman alone. Some homeless women are reported to dress like men in order to avoid detection (Golden 1992:137–138).

Another factor contributing to an underestimate of the extent of homelessness among women is the tendency to focus on the sheltered homeless. In a major study of homeless single women in England, Austerberry and Watson (1983) found that there were significantly fewer hostel (shelter) beds for women than for men; therefore confining a study of homelessness to those who are sheltered only reflects the provision of services and not the extent of the problem. For example, in 1979 the Housing Advice Switchboard (a housing advice agency for single people in England) received an equal number of single male and single female inquiries, despite the significantly fewer number of spaces for women in hostels. Another factor is that many women are what in England is referred to as "concealed" homeless (i.e., staying with friends and relatives, even if the conditions are undesirable).

This chapter will focus on the single homeless woman, in contrast to the homeless mother whose children are still with her. The term "single" may cause confusion, because in common parlance single often connotes "never married," whereas most single homeless women were married at one time, and many have had children (Austerberry and Watson 1983).

Historical Perspectives

Historical references to homeless women refer to them mainly as witches, prostitutes, and public lodging house residents. In an analysis of the relationship between witches and poverty, Keith Thomas (1971) maintains that most of the witches brought to trial in the sixteenth and seventeenth centuries were poor women to whom public relief had been denied. Thomas hypothesizes that the tendency to accuse women of being witches was an expression of the tension between the

Christian admonishment to give alms to the poor and the growing hatred of the financial burden caused by them.

The older homeless woman may be reminiscent of the archetypal witch (Golden 1992, O'Brien 1973). Through her physical appearance, her angry mutterings, and her lack of an identifiable social role, she is imbued with the connotation of evil magic. Although there may not be "hard" data supporting this connection, the taunt of "witch" is not an uncommon one for the older homeless woman in the United States.

The relationship between poverty and prostitution is well known, from the frontier days of the American West (Butler 1985) to nineteenth-century Scotland (Mahood 1990), Victorian England (Finnegan 1979), and more recently Asia (see Murray 1991, for an ethnographic account of prostitutes coming from the *kampung*, spontaneous settlements in Jakarta, Indonesia, or the work of Phongpalchit [1982] on the masseuses of Bangkok, Thailand). In England, it seems clear that some form of poverty was the major reason that girls became prostitutes (Finnegan 1979:213).

In a study of poverty in mid-nineteenth-century Europe (1968), Henry Mayhew describes the fate of an old prostitute, as he found her in a London brothel:

> We went into another room, which should more correctly be called a hole. There was not an atom of furniture in it, nor a bed and yet it contained a woman. This woman was lying on the floor, with not even a bundle of straw beneath her, wrapped up in what appeared to be a shawl, but which might have been taken for the dress of a scarecrow feloniously abstracted from a cornfield. . . . Her face was shrivelled and famine-stricken, her eyes bloodshot and glaring, her features disfigured slightly with disease, and her hair dishevelled, tangled and matted. . . . We spoke to her, and from her replies concluded she was an Irishwoman. She said she was charged nothing for the place she slept in. She cleaned out the water-closets in the daytime, and for these services she was given a lodging gratis. (232)

There are other early examples of the homeless woman in England, such as this account from eighteenth-century London:

> In 1793, six women were discovered in an empty house, three dead of starvation and two others nearly so. Two of the dead women had sheltered there for some months at least; they were both basket women who carried loads in Fleet market and were both known as Bet. The story of

the one who was still alive is typical. She was the daughter of a jeweler . . . her parents died when she was six, a neighbor took charge of her for years. She was able to get work in the silk weaving district of Spitialfields, but was discharged by her last employer, who had kept her six years when she became ill. She appealed to the church warden of her father's parish, who refused her all help and did not even tell her that she had gained a settlement in the parish where she had worked for six years. She slept in the streets till she was told of the empty house, where after lying ill for a week with ague and without food of any kind, she was helped by (one of the other women) and when she was better went out to beg. (Golden n.d., cited in Martin 1987:36)

An important element in this passage is the fact that residency in a parish had to be established before relief was granted. Laws such as the Elizabethan Poor Law of 1601 addressed themselves to vagrancy and mobility (Trattner 1989). If one could establish that a person was not from a particular locale, there was no obligation to provide assistance. Early welfare laws in England (and in the United States up until the U.S. Supreme Court decision of 1969 declaring residency requirements in determining eligibility for public assistance unconstitutional) concentrated on establishing residency and therefore responsibility for the individual, which made it easy for local governments to deny the homeless government aid.

Some sources estimate that in the United States during the Great Depression of the 1930s, as many as 30,000 women took to the road (Fennell 1974). Bertha Thompson, nicknamed Box-Car Bertha—a "sister of the road"—was one of them. In a firsthand account of riding the rails chronicled by Ben Reitman (1937), Bertha Thompson tells of her travels on the road during the 1920s and 1930s, discussing her fellow homeless women, many of whom had escaped from unhappy situations and eventually landed in Chicago.

On arrival most of them were bedraggled, dirty and hungry. Half of them were ill. There were pitiful older ones who had been riding freights all over the country with raging toothaches. . . . Some were obviously diseased, and most of them were careless about their ailments unless they had overwhelming pain. (Reitman 68–69)

A history of the Women's Emergency Shelter in New York City by Morris Chase (Bahr and Garret 1976:183–184) documents from at least

Mealtime, Female Almshouse, Blackwell's Island, circa 1897.

Museum of the City of New York. The Byron Collection.

1913 the existence of the Municipal Lodging House, which was located at East 25th Street near First Avenue. Here, food and housing were provided on a temporary basis (not to exceed five nights per month). Both men and women were admitted, but they used separate entrances to the building. During the Depression as many as 100 women per night were housed. By 1935, the women were moved to a double brownstone house, and a variety of additional sites were used. Most often it appears that unattached homeless women (who were described as alcoholics, emotionally disturbed, or transient) were separated from women with children. Efforts to move the women to better facilities most often met with opposition from those living in the neighborhoods.

Descriptions of Homeless Women

Contemporary interest in single homeless women has focused on the sheltered homeless, the elderly, and women living in street encampments. As in the case of homeless men, these women combine a picture of sickness and loneliness with one of independence and a striving to retain their dignity.

A study of 102 women hostel (shelter) residents in London in the early 1980s points to features of single life that may apply to many homeless women. The immediate reasons to enter hostels were marital or cohabiting disputes; legal and illegal evictions; requests by landlords to leave their housing; death of the tenant or owner of the housing (usually a relative or husband); and never having had secure accommodation (Austerberry and Watson 1983). These immediate causes need to be understood against the backdrop of the overwhelming lack of decent affordable housing for single people; the fact that women's wages are approximately two-thirds of men's wages; an educational system that does not encourage women to succeed or to enter higher education or training programs; and, for married women, the difficulty of trying to enter the labor market after many years of unpaid work (Austerberry and Watson 1983:6–7). All these factors lead to the hostel as the only option.

Another interesting finding with more general implications was that when a marriage broke up, it was often the woman who had to leave (in contrast to the popular myth that women retain the housing). Sometimes housing is tied to the husband's employment. For example:

> Mrs. Mount (age 53) had lived in Kenya for 23 years with her husband in services accommodation—he was in the army. The marriage then began to deteriorate, her husband frequently brought home girlfriends: "I got the boot. I was packed on the aeroplane like a brown paper parcel and sent home—England was still 'home' for me." She arrived back with no job and nowhere to go. She stayed for three months with her daughter, where there was little room, and then moved out to a hostel where she has lived for three years. (Austerberry and Watson 1983:9)

Women who have not been in the housing market for a long time frequently have no idea how difficult it is to find a new home following divorce or separation:

Mrs. Wilson for example had her own tenancy in a Peabody flat. She married and her husband moved in. Some years later the relationship broke down: "I thought that I would be able to find somewhere else, since I had never had any trouble with housing before. My husband said he would contest the divorce if I didn't let him have the flat, and I couldn't face a long drawn out case with all our problems aired publicly so I left. Peabody then transferred the flat into his name and refused to give me anywhere. I would never have left had I realised what would happen." (Austerberry and Watson 1983:11)

Some women have had "tied accommodations," that is, the accommodation is a benefit of their employment. The problem is that many of these jobs, such as nursing, require physical strength, and as they get older, these women are no longer strong enough for the work. Today, it is more difficult to find tied accommodations, as in the case of Miss West:

I lived in nurses' homes for 15 years. I moved when I changed jobs. It was easy to get places in nurses' homes then. But now even nurses, once they're qualified, can't find places in nurses' homes, they're all filled up with student nurses. While you're training you're guaranteed a place in a nurses' home, but it's become more difficult to get accommodation with the job.

Some homeless women are hidden from view and therefore difficult to describe. For example, an anthropological study of older women in France (women of the *troisième âge*, meaning the latter third of life, from 60 through 90) found that some single older women who had been abandoned by their husbands claimed to be widows (Athanas 1991). The study also found that although most poor single women lived in single-room pensions, some resorted to living on the street, seeking refuge from church sextons, who offered them rudimentary shelter.

In Toulouse, I observed a woman in her 80's spending her time in a church yard or at the train station. She carried several plastic sacks of meticulously wrapped bread and biscuit crumbs. Her left foot was swollen and wrapped with blood encrusted cloths. When I spoke to her she seemed not to be worried about her foot, but rather with packing and repacking her bags. I encountered this same woman again at the train station where she was using the mirror of a photo machine to see herself

in order to arrange her hair. Other older women I encountered were outside, actively panhandling or sitting quietly in the Paris Metro with a hat
or hand extended for donations. (Athanas 1991:7)

Our knowledge of single homeless women in the United States comes
from social surveys that operate explicitly or implicitly within the concept of *disaffiliation*, or lack of ties and interconnections with other people. In a large study in the late 1960s in New York City, Bahr and
Garrett (1976) interviewed women of 45 years and older who were living in single-room-occupancy hotels and in a women's shelter in the
neighborhood of the Bowery. The study showed how dangerous life
was for these women, who pleaded for protection against the muggings
and robbery that often were their lot. Their requests for police protection appeared to go unheeded. Many rarely left their room because of
the danger in the streets. The researchers also found the public
women's shelter to be a grim, hopeless place.

This particular study confirmed impressions of the higher-than-
normal alcohol abuse problem in this group. When fifty-two of the shelter women were asked about their drinking patterns, approximately
one-third identified themselves as heavy drinkers, one-third as moder-
ate, and one-third as very light or abstainers. An interesting finding was
that the women's self-reported drinking corresponded with the quantity–frequency index developed by Bahr and Garrett, whereas the men
in their study consistently underrated (either deluding themselves
about the amount of alcohol they actually consumed or deliberately
lying about it) the extent of their drinking.

Large-scale studies of homelessness are sometimes useful in
understanding characteristics of homeless women. For example,
Martha R. Burt and Barbara E. Cohen of the Urban Institute (1989) led
a research team that interviewed 1,704 homeless people in twenty
cities in the United States in March 1987. The respondents included
single homeless men, single homeless women, and homeless women
with children. The interviews took place in both shelters and soup
kitchens. The inclusion of soup kitchens enabled the research to take
into account a sizable number of the unsheltered homeless living on
the streets. The shelters and soup kitchens, as well as the individual
homeless people seeking assistance at them, were randomly drawn
samples, making this one of the few studies from which generaliza-

tions can be applied to homeless people in places other than the area of study. The large numbers also allowed the researchers to answer the question of how these three groups of homeless people (men, women, and women with children) differ from each other, and consequently, how their needs vary.

In general, Burt and Cohen found that homeless women with children differ more from single homeless women (who may be mothers but whose children are no longer with them) than homeless men and women differ from each other. They also found that services and facilities for homeless families were the largest growing types of services in the United States in the 1980s, in contrast to services for single men or women. Burt and Cohen estimated that 194,000 homeless adults used soup kitchens and shelters in the large U.S. cities in March 1987. Of these, 73 percent were single men, 9 percent were single women, and another 9 percent were women accompanied by at least one child (1989:511). They learned that 59 percent of the single homeless women were nonwhite (in contrast to 83 percent of the women with children and 52 percent of the single men), and that they were the best educated of the three groups.

Individual single women had been homeless for an average of 34 months (closer to the 43 months of the single men than the 15 months of the women with children). They had the least number of months of recent joblessness (41 months, in contrast to the 46 months of the women with children and 50 months for the homeless men). Interestingly, Burt and Cohen observed that time spent without a job was longer on average than time spent without shelter, suggesting that joblessness preceded homelessness and contributed to it.

Social Network Perspective

In contrast to the disaffiliation perspective, which inquires into the lack of relationships, the social network perspective focuses on homeless people's formal and nonformal associations. In a study in and around Los Angeles's skid row, Rowe and Wolch charted the social networks and daily paths of homeless women in order to understand how they survived living outdoors (1990). The women appeared to derive their emotional support through relationships with men (who offered them protection) and with other homeless people. If they lived in a street encampment (examples are Justiceville and Love Camp), they had a base from which to operate. They could leave the camp feeling that their belongings would be watched over.

Some women relied on panhandling, which they found satisfying because it served as an alternative to relying solely on public assistance. They also participated in social relationships, which offered the potential for some reciprocity, as the following case illustrates:

> Lisa: There's a guy that comes from Loma Linda every Sunday, a 93-year-old that I met here one day. I asked him for some change, and he says, "Can you write?" . . . And I wrote a letter to his daughter. . . . And that's got to be a thing I did every Sunday for him. I got lunch and five dollars from him for writing a few letters. . . . And last Sunday he was real upset because he's been low on cash. He says, "I don't have any money to give you." "Arthur, that's ok, no problem," I said. (Rowe and Wolch 1990:196)

A woman receiving governmental assistance can occasionally find a sympathetic ear and get some tangible help from the people who handle her case, but more often, she is transferred from case worker to case worker. She is often treated impersonally, and the bureaucratic requirements of public assistance (for example, having all one's paper work in order) are extremely difficult. Further, eligibility for public assistance (most often General Assistance for single people) is based on a week-to-week assessment. Since landlords know this, they are often reluctant to rent to people on public assistance, because they might soon become ineligible. Some homeless prefer the emotional support and sense of community in the encampment over returning to the mainstream (Rowe and Wolch 1990).

A study of social networking in England (Mitchell 1987) suggests at least two patterns of social relationships among homeless women. In the first pattern a women becomes homeless when her marriage breaks up and she must seek shelter elsewhere; her social network is confined to the social workers and other women at the refuge. In the second pattern, a woman comes to the hostel with her husband and children. She has strong links to both her own kin and her husband's kin; both sides of the family have strong links to each other. The study was able to contrast the stronger relationships of the woman still living within her own household, albeit in a shelter, with those of the woman alone.

Survival Strategies

There are indications that like men, some homeless women survive through begging (also known as panhandling). There are also inferences that they exchange sex for money. However, as yet there is no reliable evidence of any broad pattern of such behavior.

Health Issues

Life on the streets can have especially devastating consequences for homeless women in terms of their health. In the United States, single homeless women comprise the largest percentage of those reporting being in fair or poor health (44 percent, in contrast to 40 percent of women with children and 33 percent of men in one study [Burt and Cohen 1989]). One-fourth of single women report having been hospitalized for mental illness, in contrast with one-fifth of the men and fewer than one-tenth of the women with children (although even the one-fourth figure for mental hospitalization is lower than the popular conception of the relationship between homelessness and mental illness [Burt and Cohen 1989]).

In the Health Care for the Homeless Program (Wright and Weber 1987), it was found that homeless men are at greater risk for tuberculosis, hypertension, and all categories of trauma, and that homeless women show higher rates of eating and nutritional disorders, endocrinological disorders, and genitourinary disorders. There was a 10 percent pregnancy rate among the homeless women, and the rate of sexually transmitted diseases was 2 percent (in contrast to 1.4 percent for the men). The overall finding of this research was that homeless people are significantly more ill than their counterparts in the general population, suffering from higher mortality rates and a greater number of serious disorders.

Homeless people often must rely for food on "emergency" programs such as soup kitchens and meals provided at shelters. In North America, these programs are no longer "emergency" in nature, in that for many homeless people they represent most of their food intake. When soup kitchen and shelter meals are evaluated according to the health needs of the homeless, they are found often to fall short in terms of nutritional standards. For example, in a nutritional study of homeless women in Canada, a random sample of eighty-four single homeless women were interviewed (Bunston and Breton 1990). The majority (85 percent) of the women said that they relied on hostels (shelters) and drop-in centers for their food. When the women's food intake for four food groups (meat and meat alternatives, milk and milk products, breads and cereals, and fruits and vegetables) was compared with the Canadian Food Guide recommendations, the women's average number of servings of each of the food groups was below the recommended amounts. If the providers (both staff and volunteers) of these food programs appreciated the extent to which the homeless relied on them, they might devote more attention to the content of the meals and improve the overall health of the homeless.

Programs and Policies for Homeless Women

As in the case of homeless men, programs for homeless women range from daytime refuges for getting off the street to housing with a supportive environment.

In Montreal, Chez Doris is a daytime refuge for "itinerant women." In Quebec, itinerant is a word that, in contrast to the word homeless (or *sans-abri*), stresses a transient life-style rather than a lack of housing. It also has the advantage of being the same word in French and English and, as such, fits the needs of a bilingual community.

> Chez Doris, a day centre for women, was founded in 1977 by a group of community workers and other interested individuals who took to heart the poignant request of an alcoholic prostitute named Doris. Doris was often heard to say that she wished there was a place for women to get together for a cup of coffee and a bit of conversation safe from prying do-gooders and demanding male pimps and alcoholics. Doris was brutally murdered in 1974, so was never able to benefit from the many services offered at Chez Doris. . . . Chez Doris is an island of safety in an otherwise violent world. (Chez Doris, informational packet for volunteers, 1992:2)

Chez Doris accommodates approximately fifty women a day, who can rest, eat, take a bath, do laundry, converse, read, play games, and occasionally go on trips together. The staff is instructed to be available and helpful, but to respect their right to live as they want to live, and not to require anything of them (Day 1992). A well-stocked clothing bank downstairs offers the women secondhand clothing in good condition that is appropriate for the season. Chez Doris appears to be a model in nonobtrusive services for women of the street. It has been found that soup kitchens, shelters, and refuges that impose few demands tend to attract the greatest number of people (Glasser 1992b).

Another approach to assisting homeless women is the attempt to build companionable relationships and a sense of community through social group work (Martin and Nayowith 1988). For example, the Manhattan Bowery Corporation (MBC) administers the Midtown Outreach Program, which offers the mentally ill homeless access to services. In one of its activities, homeless women were able to feel comfortable with one another and with medical and psychiatric staff in a drop-in center setting.

> At an MBC drop-in center for homeless women, considered the first step off the street, women came to sit in chairs throughout the day and night, receive food, clothing, and other social service support. The MBC medical/psychiatric team members noticed that several of the women discussed current events raised by newspaper articles or television shows. They decided to build on the informal group in order to develop a time limited formal group activity with a goal of introducing themselves and the services of the team to the women. The women were intrigued by the newspaper activity and the opportunity to talk together with workers about many topics of interest. Subsequently the members brought other homeless women for participation in the group as well as in the MBC health/mental health clinic program. (Martin and Nayowith 1988:85–86)

Similar first steps toward communication were developed with mentally ill women living in single-room-occupancy (SRO) housing who had been on the street and were in danger of going back. Two groups described by Martin and Nayowith are the "bingo" group (with, as the women said, "free food and prizes even if you don't win") and the cooking group. Although the groups are directed by social work professionals, the women are responsible for doing the jobs that the activities require. In the case of the "cooking" group, the dinners (and cooking) continued without the assistance of staff members.

In Toronto, the drop-in center called Sistering provides individual and group support for women on the streets:

For homeless women who must be out of the hostels during the daytime (which is the general rule), the drop-in provides a roof over their heads, a warm, clean and dry place to sit and rest their feet without getting hassled, and a space where they can sleep if they have been walking all night, or if the noise, the crowding and the stealing which regularly goes on in some of the hostels have kept them awake. Some food is provided: there is a constant supply of coffee, tea and soup supplied by a local merchant since the beginning of the program. (Breton 1988:49)

Unlike many services for the homeless that are physically set apart from the rest of the population, Sistering is part of a community center offering recreational and educational activities to the nonhomeless population. This "normalization" aspect demands that the women follow some basic rules of behavior.

After a short trial-and-error period, it was established that there would be no physical fights and no prolonged screaming and carrying-on: definite time-limits now exist for "blowing-up," and consequences of refusing to conform to behavioral expectations are enforced, albeit with compassion—the women have to leave the room and the Centre temporarily. (Breton 1988:52)

The work at the Sistering drop-in center emphasizes the need to balance the help offered to the women individually with the desire of the drop-in center leadership for the women to form mutual aid groups. The concept of mutual aid groups reflects the tradition of liberation theology, which stresses that the women need to start to see their plight collectively (e.g., homelessness as a result of the feminization of poverty and the inadequacy of the programs for the deinstitutionalized population) rather than as their individual failing.

The modest amount of research regarding homeless women is by and large confined to the industrialized world. In the developing world, homeless women primarily mean women with children. It is impossible to know with certainty whether this lack of research is due to an absence of single homeless women or is an outgrowth of the conceptualizations of homelessness, which have been male dominated. Successful research on the single homeless woman is the result of intense ethnographic study (as in the case of Athanas in France, who concentrated on the older woman) or participatory projects such as Chez Doris (Montreal) or the Mid-Town Outreach Program

(Manhattan). Because the single woman has learned to stay in the shadows in order to survive, her plight has also tended to remain hidden from view. Further studies, especially those that are cross-cultural or global in scope, would do much to contribute to our understanding of the single homeless woman.

4

Homeless Children

A grubby eight-year-old boy was sitting on the floor of the YMCA in Kingston, Jamaica, covered in scars from knife fights with other boys in the park where he spent his nights. He worked at a busy traffic intersection, wiping car windscreens to get the cash for his survival—and for gambling with other street boys. In his right hand he held the filthy rag he used. The thumb of his other hand was stuck firmly in his mouth. (Ennew 1986:10)

In this single image of a little boy sucking his thumb for comfort while trying to survive without the protection of parents or responsible adults, the basic incongruity of children on the street is captured.

Compared to homeless men and homeless women, we know much about homeless children from many parts of the world. Perhaps this is not surprising in that the very idea of homeless children is an assault on what we know about the needs of all children. In the countries of the developing world the most frequent organizing term used for research is "street children," with the related concerns of child labor, begging, and child prostitution. In the United States, the term "homeless children" most often implies children living with their mothers in shelters. In Eastern Europe, the reference is usually to children who have been abandoned and are living in institutions. In various parts of the world, the term "homeless youth" (usually referring in age to post-puberty) most often means children living on their own, outside of institutions.

Some of our best information about street children comes from the street educators, contact workers, and counselors who are in daily contact with the children through street schools and centers. The information provided by these workers, sometimes based on participatory research, reflects the time and effort it takes to earn the trust of the children. Vivid newspaper reports can also provide us with firsthand material, as the following excerpt from Johannesburg illustrates:

> The grimy cotton quilt on the sidewalk looked like a heap of discarded rags until it began to wriggle. In the dim glow of a street lamp, two 13-year-old vagabonds, Zani and Sipho, crawled from their makeshift bed.
>
> Sipho said he had run away from Katlebong, a black township a dozen miles away. Zani said he drifted in from Newcastle, 240 miles distant, in Natal. They were what are known in Zulu as "malunde," children living wild in South African cities, as the ultimate discards of apartheid.
>
> Hundreds of street children haunt Hillbrow, a racially mixed Johannesburg neighborhood of honky-tonks, ethnic restaurants and decaying apartment buildings. They submit to what they refer to in their offhand slang as "chop-chop," sexual molestation by cruising pedophiles who give them unaccustomed affection and enough for a meal afterward. Or they beg, filch and hustle to get spare change for bread and video games. (Wren 1991:A4)

Types of Street Children

The Inter-NGO (Non-Governmental Organization) Programme on Street Children defines the street child as

> any girl or boy who has not reached adulthood, for whom the street—in the widest sense of the word, including unoccupied dwellings, wasteland, etc. has become his/her habitual abode and/or source of livelihood and who is inadequately protected, supervised or directed by responsible adults. (Inter-NGO Programme on Street Children and Street Youth 1983:24)

A widely used typology of street children developed by UNICEF (1986) suggests two major categories of homeless/street children: children *on* the street, who work on the streets during the day and return home most nights; and children *of* the streets, who work and sleep on the streets, maintaining minimal contact with their families. Children on the street may spend a portion or all of their day working in the informal economy, for example, selling flowers, begging, guarding cars, or shining shoes. Their parents are likely near by, and the children may sleep at home every night or at least on a regular basis. Children of the street have only occasional contact with their family. They may have started out working on the streets and then run away from home because of family problems. Often their family links deteriorate the longer they stay on the street (Jones 1991). A third category, used by the street child advocacy agency CHILDHOPE, is the truly abandoned or orphaned child whose life revolves entirely around the street and whose only reference group is made up of other street children. CHILDHOPE estimates that 75 percent of the world's street children are those "on" the street, 20 percent are those "of" the street, and 5 percent are truly abandoned street children with no family ties (Rocky 1989).

Although many discussions throughout the world blur these distinctions among homeless children, they are important. For example, in

In the "Sun" Pressroom at 2 AM, circa 1888.

The Jacob A. Riis Collection, #182. Museum of the City of New York.

estimating the numbers of homeless children, one cannot simply look on the street and count the children. Also, some street workers stress that by ignoring any remnants of family ties, outsiders relinquish a potential source of help for the children. Since children move from one category to another, careful research can help to assess whether children who are working on the street at a given time may be drifting to living there too. Good preventive work could be undertaken that addresses itself to helping the family support itself economically so that they can survive with their child at home.

Numbers and Gender

It is difficult to estimate the true number of homeless children in the world. One widely cited estimate, supported by UNICEF, suggests a figure of one hundred million street children (Irvine 1991, Ennew 1990). This number includes children who work on the street (ca. 71 million), children who mostly work and live on the street (ca. 23 million), and abandoned children (ca. 7 million) (Ennew 1990).

A hidden but significant number of abandoned children live in institutions. For example, in Brazil the Foundation for Welfare of Minors (FUNABEM) reports that there are 555,873 minors in government-related institutions. The majority are children of poor families who cannot support them (Sanders 1987:7).

The number of girls who are street children tends to be underestimated significantly, according to reports from CHILDHOPE (Ward 1987). For example, a study from the Philippines reported approximately 19 percent of the children on the street to be female (Silva 1987, as cited in Ward 1987). A similar study in Asunción, Paraguay, reported approximately 12 percent to be female (Espinola 1987, as cited in Ward 1987). However, because these studies looked at the traditionally masculine street occupations of shining shoes and minding cars and did not include children working in the market or those exploited in prostitution, they ignored significant numbers of girls.

Historical Perspectives

> The most pitiful victims of the tragedy that Russia has lived through since the revolution have been the little children. . . . Dressed in rags

Street Arabs, Barelegged; Mulberry Street, circa 1890.

The Jacob A. Riis Collection, #122. Museum of the City of New York.

and starving, the poor little creatures wander the streets of the larger
Russian towns, especially Moscow, and like ferocious little animals seeking their prey, form themselves into bands. Then, in well-lit streets, they
stop the passers-by to beg, but in lonelier and darker spots, they threat-
en and attack.

They have no home, but lodge in any hole—in gutters and drains, and
in the ruins of tumble-down houses—while at night they cluster round
the huge cauldrons where the asphalt for paving the streets is heated.
(Zenzinov 1931:1–2)

Russia has had many problems with homeless children. One of the most
famous instances of homeless children occurred during the period from
World War I (1914) through the famine of 1921, when it is estimated
that as many as five million children, after being deserted by or separated from their parents, were forced to beg on the streets of the large
cities or sent to institutions (Zenzinov 1931:70).

There is ample visual and literary evidence of the existence of homeless children in North America and Western Europe. The paintings and,

later, the photographs, of the nineteenth-century United States present us with numerous portrayals of homeless children, ranging in point of view from the idealized sentimental paintings of newspaper boys, shoeshine boys, and street sweepers to the brutally realistic photographs of Jacob Riis and Lewis Hine (Peters 1987). In 1868 *The New York Times* estimated that there were 20,000 street children in the city, whom they described as "'wharf rats,' petty thieves and squalid beggars," deploring the fact that a city as wealthy as New York could not afford to rescue these children (Peters 1987:52).

Descriptions of Homeless Children

There are many descriptions of street children, some of whose own words have been recorded to communicate their story. While the vignettes that follow focus on different locales around the world, they also point to some general worldwide patterns.

Becoming a Child of the Street

The path to the street for a child tends to be a gradual one. In one story, Peter Taçon, UNICEF regional advisor for the Abandoned and Street Children Project of Bogotá, Colombia, recounts the life of Luis Carlos, who appears to exemplify the journey to the street of many of the children of Latin America. Taçon was leaving his hotel room in Porto Alegre, Brazil, in order to get a breath of air after attending a banquet of local officials:

> As I crossed the main central city intersection, I noticed a crumpled and ragged figure crouching on the curb on the opposite corner. He was rubbing his eyes and spitting into the gutter. Filthy and alone, he was a candidate for abandonment to be sure!
>
> He appeared to be about 7 years old (he was actually 11), and as I approached him, he stood up and came to see me with the sad countenance and outstretched palm of the trained street kid who learns to inspire pity if his begging is to be successful. He limped and stooped slightly to add legitimacy to his performance. Instead of paying off the boy and my conscience, I spoke a few words to him and settled on the curb myself. After carefully assessing me, he joined me.
>
> I guess I had heard his story in Bogotá, San José, Managua, Mexico

and Lima a thousand times before—moved from the country to the city, father left, mother took up with one and then another stepfather, the latter of whom had beaten the living daylights out of him, no food at home, seven brothers and sisters (he was the oldest boy), a final fight in the slum shack of a home, tears, kicking, blood . . . and he was out! But what was little Luis Carlos doing in downtown Porto Alegre!

"I had no place to go once I left the vila [neighborhood]. Nobody gives a damn there about the son of a whore who's been booted out of the home. There are lots of us. The only person I still have in the world is my father; he'd never turn me away; he's a good guy and he works down here somewhere in one of the plants or on the docks or something."

"But your father left you and your family. How long ago was that?" I countered.

"Oh, Paizinho took off about five years ago, but he had to then. He couldn't get work and we kids were driving him crazy. But he's been back to visit us, and he's told us to look him up if ever any one of us boys gets into trouble."

Good Lord, I thought, what had I come upon—the classic collage of every little kid's life I'd ever known. I suggested we continue our talk as we moved towards a food vendor who was still open near the central park, and I asked myself why Luis Carlos had not been invited to our banquet: there had been far too much food there. Like a piranha he devoured something that resembled a cheese sandwich and a chunk of tough beef, talking all the time—about how he's gone to school but had dropped out of grade one after the third try in order to work and look after his little brothers and sisters, how he'd been beaten up and had his quota stolen several times by the older kids of his vila, and how his mother needed an operation and was always crying, how he slept on the floor, how the roof leaked, how the house stank, etc., etc. On and on he plunged into the dark past of his 11 years on an unfriendly planet, not resentful of what life had done to him, just wishing things had been and would be better. He was going to find his father, and that would cure everything. He would never go back home to the vila—never.

Then, as I got up to return to my hotel (after all, I had to be rested for the next day, and what could I do anyway), little Luis Carlos grabbed my forearm. "Take me with you; I won't be a problem. I'm cold; take me to Canada." I puzzled over the irony of "I'm cold; take me to Canada," but more than anything I was trying to figure out how I could work out a space in the life of my family for Luis Carlos. I knew it was impossible, and I told him so. I gave him a little money for breakfast the next day, and wept inside as I told him I was sorry, and that I had to go now. Like so many others before me, I was passing him by—and Luis Carlos knew it. But I hope he knew that I cared too.

By the time I looked . . . at him for the last time, he was beginning to cross the park. He turned, and with a grin he cried, "I'm off now; I know that my father's here somewhere." (Taçon 1984a:5)

The story of Luis Carlos illustrates the themes of rural to urban migration, poverty, a stepparent, interrupted schooling, and finally, a life on the streets. It also presents the quandary of the middle-class person when confronted with the unfortunate circumstances of someone like Luis Carlos, as well as the boy's basic hopefulness.

When children are asked why they are living on the streets, many

Boys smoking, Brazil.

UNICEF/Claudio Edinger.

say that they are working to help out their family. This was the conclusion of a study of street children from Rio, the Amazonian city of Belém, and the northeastern city of Teresina in Brazil (Sanders 1987:7). After working on the streets all day, most of the children returned home to sleep with their families, although those in Rio slept outside on some nights, because they could not afford to return to their homes outside of the city. The study suggests that children working on the streets of Brazilian cities is an urban continuation of the tradition of Brazil's rural poor children working to help maintain the family. An interesting footnote to the research from Brazil is that many of the children (55 percent in Rio, 65 percent in Teresina, and 82 percent in Belém) claimed to be attending school, although they were primarily interviewed on the street during school hours.

The *Khate* of Nepal and the Parking Boys of Kenya

The words used for street children often reflect the jobs they do. For example, the *khate* in Kathmandu, Nepal, are ragpickers who survive by collecting and reselling trash (Child Workers in Nepal Concerned Center 1990). The word *khate* means "the one born to eat" in Nepali (*Voice of Child Workers* 1990). A *khate* works ten hours a day, collecting trash from roadside dumping areas and riverbanks.

> The Khate in Kathmandu are mostly the migrant children from the country sides who have come to the capital to earn easy money and live better and who have found themselves facing the harsh reality stripped of their rosy dreams. Majority of these children coming to Kathmandu first get employed in small tea shops, poor urban restaurants where having to work as much as 17 hours a day, that too accompanied by abuses from masters and big bully at work place, these boys tend to run away from the work before the first 2 months without due wage of course. Once in the street and empty pocket, they sooner or later start scavenging which is the only handy work they can do besides begging. Of 105 street children in CWIN Common Room 90% have this story to tell. Khate spends their nights sleeping inside junkyards, old garages, at construction sites, on temples and on street pavements. (*Voice of Child Workers* 1990:24)

A portion of the children eventually turn to stealing *maal*, which consists of plastic, scraps of metal, paper, and bottles. The Child Workers in Nepal Concerned Center (CWIN) estimates that 90 percent of the street children in Kathmandu will end up in detention centers, accused of stealing, as well as for begging in public places, sleeping on the pavement, and trying to bribe the police.

Out of 100 children interviewed, forty-eight had come to Kathmandu from rural villages either by themselves or with friends; thirteen were squatter children who worked during the day and returned home at night; and thirty-nine were orphaned or abandoned children, who may have experienced physical and mental abuse and did not know the whereabouts of their parents or stepparents. In CWIN's research the proportion of orphaned or abandoned children was higher than the UNICEF estimates of only 5 percent for street children worldwide.

Another group of street children are the "parking boys" of Nairobi, Kenya, who are so named because one of their jobs is guarding the cars of people in the city. Parking boys are most often the children of formerly rural families who have moved to the squatter settlements of the city (Schenk 1991). One former parking boy, Tony Kamande, tells his story:

> I ran away from my parent's home on a coffee estate near the village of Thika when I was 13 or 14. My parents were squatters. My father drank all the time. Sometimes my mother drank, and they always fought. I was strong-willed and disobedient. Finally, I left.
>
> In Nairobi there was no place I could afford to live, so I came to the Mathare Valley and fell in with young boys who stole anything. We slept in drainage ditches and garbage bins. We'd get up early in the morning and try to find some scraps of wood or an abandoned tire that we could burn for warmth.
>
> Older boys often used us to set up victims in the streets for theft. They would force us to help or they'd extort what money we stole. We made money watching parked cars for the drivers, but if they didn't pay us to watch their cars we broke into them and stole whatever we could.
>
> At that age I was drinking *changaa* (illicit home-brewed alcohol), sniffing petrol and smoking cigarettes and opium. If I tried going home to my parents in Thika they would beat me. So I stayed away. (Schenk 1991:11)

Tony escaped from the street when he joined the Redeemed Gospel Church. This led to working at Canaanland, a drug rehabilitation center sponsored by World Vision of Germany and the Redeemed Gospel Church. At Canaanland, Tony and other former parking boys work with forty to fifty boys a day, providing them with counseling, taking them on educational field trips, and enrolling some in vocational training programs.

Gamines of Colombia

In 1970 the psychoanalyst José Gutiérrez (1970) identified the word *gamino/a* as coming from the French word *gamin* and concluded that it had been used in Colombia for at least thirty years. To attain the full meaning of the word, it is generally spoken in a particular way: "the reader might try pronouncing it with a tone of voice combining fear and disgust, uneasiness and weary fatalism generally reserved for natural disaster, much as in medieval times one might have said 'the plague'" (Gutiérrez 1972b:45).

A 1990 estimate suggests that 5,000 gamines live on the streets of Bogotá, and 1,000 on the streets of Cali (Felsman 1981). Gaminismo has been linked to a rural to urban migration exacerbated by the period of rural political violence known as La Violencia from the 1940s through the 1960s.

Kirk Felsman identifies three types of gamines. One, there are children who spend the vast majority of the daytime in the streets "working," but return home each night. For example:

> Carmen (age 6), Elena (age 5) and Maria (la niña or "the baby") are sisters who beg together within a circumscribed number of blocks in downtown Cali, appearing at the same open air restaurant every morning. I was struck from the outset by the contrast between their joyful play among themselves and the sad tale they recited together while "working." Coached by her older sisters, cowering a little, hands outstretched, Maria was always the first to approach a stranger and begin to tell their story. Over the months, I came to know them—and their mother. She was not in a home for the destitute, where her daughters' story placed her, but only a few blocks way, working as a fruit vendor. Mother and daughters traveled daily from the squatter settlement where they lived to Cali's downtown areas. The girls would then leave their mother to beg on their own, but they would check in with her periodically and return home with her at night. (Felsman 1981:43)

The second type is characterized by abandoned children who have no home and spend almost all of their time on the streets, including nights.

The third type is made up of children who have run away from home, as in the case of Jorge:

> Not yet ten, Jorge is a veteran of the streets. He believes his family is still in Buenaventura, Colombia's busy southern port, but has never been back to find out. "There wasn't any food to eat, so somebody had to leave." Over time, more is revealed, and particular scars are related to beatings he received from his stepfather. . . . Jorge's only attempt to fight back, striking his target with a well-aimed stone, was his last battle; he was warned never to return. . . . (Felsman 1981:43)

Groups of gamine children live in *galladas*, bands of five to fifty children with varying degrees of social organization (Maxwell 1991). Each night, the *galladas* sleep in specific locations known as their *camada*. The gang hierarchy includes a leader, known as a *perro* (dog), who decides what each member will do to earn money. Aptekar (1988) suggests that these gangs represent a substitute family, providing psychological benefits for the children.

Gamine children may move frequently between living with a family, life on the streets, and being placed in an institution. The following comments from a gamino testify to the frequent moves:

> Between living in the house and in the streets and in the institution, the best is in the institution, because here I get food and clothes. What happens is that at times one gets bored; one gets bored at times in any place. For me, I always have this circle, or better said, I go to an institution and I go to the streets and I return home. . . . The best of life on the streets is that a person can stay with the *gallada*; that is delightful, but the worst is that there are people who beat up on a person. What is bad about the home is that parents beat us up. . . . I don't know where I will end up. I leave from the house and I go to the street and then I come to the institution, and then I leave from there—this is my street life. (Muñoz and Pachón 1980:95)

Rural Homelessness

Homelessness among children does not occur only in an urban setting. In one report from Peru, children leave home to work in the jungle, panning for gold.

Alex Tite Huarwaya had just turned 13 last March when he left his Andean home . . . and came to this frontier outpost deep in the Amazon to seek his fortune panning for gold.

But like thousands of children trucked into the Peruvian jungle every year, recruited by shady employment agencies in their hometown with promises of riches, Alex saw no glitter. . . .

"We have children as young as 12 coming here in very large numbers," said Victor Raul Solorio, regional director of the Labor Department. "They work 9 to 12 hours a day, not getting paid, malnourished, many eventually die from disease. They are so isolated that they can't escape."

Alex said that for the equivalent of $2.60 a day, he stood ankle deep in water holding a large plastic pipe, hosing down rocks and sand in a process referred to here as gold washing. His meals, provided by the mine's owner, consisted of rice, potatoes, yucca root, and water. At night, he slept in the open air, guarding the mine's machines. (Nash 1991: A8)

Children in Homeless Shelters and Welfare Hotels

There is a great deal of both descriptive and quantitative research regarding children living in welfare hotels and homeless shelters in the United States. Estimates of the number of homeless children in the United States range from 100,000 to 750,000 (Shulsinger 1990). An elusive number of children live with their families in cramped apartments with other families, a phenomenon commonly referred to as "doubling up."

Common to welfare hotels and shelters around the world are the danger and physical inadequacy of most of these facilities. The following are some children's accounts of their days in welfare hotels:

Doreen: We stayed one night in a hotel in the Bronx, the Prospect. It was awful. There was a hole in the wall big enough for a person to walk through. There was blood on the sheets and bugs on the soap. All we could do was throw a blanket over the top of the wall to cover the hole, and we slept there because it was too late to go somewhere else.

Shama: The first time we went to our room, I was so scared to go in. I said, "Oh, my God!" I was holding on to my mother—we just followed her around. There were mattresses on the beds with mice feces on them.

No sheets or anything. It was late, like 12 o'clock, and we just stayed on the beds because we couldn't go anywhere. It was so tiny and yucky. It was so dirty. You wouldn't want to be there.

I remember that a security guard kept asking me these weird questions. I didn't know if he was teasing me or not. He kept asking me, "Where can I buy happiness?" He was serious too. . . . He would say, "I want a bag, I want a pound. I want the white kind. What color do you have?" I was like, "What is he talking about?" He went on and on. (Berck 1992:30)

Shelters are very difficult places in which to live. When many families, all under stress, are placed together in cramped spaces, conflicts often result.

Jose: There's one water fountain on each floor, and one pay telephone. There's a laundry, but you have to sign up for it the night before. They only have a couple washers and dryers for everybody, and they break a lot. People get in big fights over doing the laundry.

Maria P.: Most guards are men, even though most of the parents are mothers. Some of them would look at you like they wanted you. I really hated that.

Tasha: It's really crazy. If you got seven kids and one gets sick, all your kids got to go with you to the hospital. You can't leave them here with somebody. (Berck 1992:31)

Institutions

An unknown number of children who are abandoned by their parents are placed in institutions. In Eastern Europe the rate of institutionalization has been significantly higher than in Western Europe. In Western Europe the number of children in institutions is usually under 1 percent of the total number of children, whereas in Romania the figure is between 2.4 and 3.4 percent (Cornia and Sipos 1991). Generally, these Eastern European institutions serve children who are disabled and/or abandoned. In Hungary, research revealed institutions to have very low-quality buildings and equipment; low professional qualifications for the staff; aggressive, authoritarian educational attitudes and harsh physical penalties; and high rates of juvenile delinquency among the children. Hungarian institutions were also found to release the children at age 16, without supervision or proper preparation for the outside world (Ranschburg 1990).

In Romania, after the fall of Ceausescu in 1989, a black-market industry emerged, as Americans, Canadians, and Western Europeans went to Romania to search for and adopt abandoned children in the country's well-publicized orphanages. However, as Kathleen Hunt reveals in a 1991 article, most of the adoptions did not take place from the institutions but directly from Romanian people's homes. In fact, few of the institutionalized children were available for adoption (and the Westerners did not appear to want children with disabilities or those who tested positive for hepatitis B or HIV). The selling of babies and children by many impoverished Romanians was a way for them to gain capital.

The phenomenon of parents sending away children they cannot care for is not uncommon in some cultures. In a study in a squatter settlement in Porto Alegre, Brazil, Fonseca (1986) found that 50 percent of the fifty-four mothers over the age of 20 had at some time sent one of their children away to live with someone else, and that about one-third of these children went to the state orphanages—called the Fundacao Estadual para Bem-Estar do Menor (FEBEM). Of the seventy households in the study, sixteen had had some member living in FEBEM. Giving a child to FEBEM was part of a pattern of child circulation, which served as a kind of safety valve when the mother could no longer take care of her child (upon the arrival of a new husband, for instance). Although maternal relatives or godparents of a child were most women's first choice, the state institution was often the only alternative.

Homeless Youth

(London: January 8) Their faces still have a youthful plumpness. But Michelle and James are grey with cold and grime, and crumpled from lack of sleep. . . .

It is 9 am on a cold, wet Friday morning and they are huddled in a doorway as commuters, hardened to the sight of slumped derelicts, hurry by. They have two hours to kill before a day centre for the homeless opens its door to provide warmth, washing facilities and cheap meals. (Mills 1990)

Child on the street, Mexico.

UNICEF/Peter Taçon.

In most places in the world, the category of homeless youth is sub-
sumed under "homeless children." When homeless youth are discussed as a separate group, the age range is 11 to 25 years
(Rotheram-Borus, Koopman, and Ehrhardt 1991). Some authors make
distinctions between runaways (those who leave home without their
parent's consent), throwaways (those forced to leave), system kids
(those leaving social service system placements, such as foster care or

group homes), and street youths (those who sleep on the street) (Rotheram-Borus, Koopman, and Ehrhardt 1991). For example, a "runaway/homeless" dichotomy exists in Wales, where young people under 16 years of age are viewed as runaways, since legally they cannot leave home without parental consent, but those 16 and over are called homeless (Hutson and Liddiard 1991b). In most countries, however, distinctions (e.g., throwaways, runaways) tend to blur and overlap. Many of the case studies of homeless youth and children present situations in which the family appears to send implicit messages to the young person (through physical abuse or neglect) to leave until the child finally runs away.

A study in North Staffordshire, England, from April 1990 to March 1991, found that over 2,000 youth approached agencies for housing, and 45 percent of these were "immediately homeless" (Smith and Gilford 1991). In Canada, it is estimated that over half of the homeless of Toronto are youth between the ages of 18 and 25 (*Toronto Star* 1989).

In a major study of homeless youth (ages 16 to under 25) in Wales, Susan Hutson and Mark Liddiard (1991b) interviewed 115 homeless youth, as well as sixty-eight statutory and voluntary agencies with which they were involved. The majority of the young people became homeless when they were evicted from their own house or had to leave state care. They entered an increasingly poor housing market with a dearth of affordable rents, due to the significant reduction in public-sector housing, and a long-term decline in private rentals.

The respondents' stories elucidate the routes to homelessness. Stephen, age 17, relates how his parents told him to leave; Susan, age 16, how she left on her own; and Louise, age 17, how state care failed her:

Stephen: They [his parents] said that they'd been talking to the police and they said the law was that I could be thrown out at the age of 17. So they said: "Well, we've had to keep you for 8 months longer than we should have, so it's time to get out like. Get your stuff in the morning!" (Hutson and Liddiard 1991b:23)

Susan: It was in the summer that we had the argument and I just couldn't handle it . . . the atmosphere in the house. So I just didn't even pack my bags, I just went. . . . Well, I stayed awake all night. I walked around and then I slept in the park behind this builder's merchants. . . . (Hutson and Liddiard 1991b:24)

Louise: When I was 12 my mum beat me up so they took me into care. I went to live with a foster parent for 3 months but the lady was having a baby. . . . Then other foster parents. . . . She'd never fostered before. . . . Then my social worker got a letter from my father who I'd never seen since I was 3. . . . I moved down (to live with him) but we never got on. . . . In the end, I ran away. . . . I stayed with my friend for 4 months but her parents

TABLE 4.1. Diagrammatic representation of the *main* accommodation types used by the Welsh sample through five stages of homelessness.

ACCOMMODATION TYPE % experienced	INITIAL HOMELESSNESS		LATER HOMELESSNESS		
Staying with friends 50%	●	●	●	●	●
Staying with relatives 27%	●				
Returning to family 35%		●			
Private flat/bedsit 51%	●	●	●	●	
Bed and breakfast 27%	●	●	●	●	●
Youth residential project 44%	●	●	●		
Trad. homelessness hostel 24%			●	●	●
Squatting 14%			●	●	●
Prison 21%			●	●	●
Sleeping rough 47%	●	●	●	●	●

Susan Hutson and Mark Liddiard, *Young and Homeless in Wales*. Swansea: The School of Social Studies, University College of Swansea, 1991, p. 38.

were going through a divorce. . . . I went to live with my step-sister with 3 children. . . . Then she (social worker) got me a place in the host scheme but the landlady there . . . we antagonized each other. . . . If I were to live my life again, I wouldn't have it happen. I'd want proper parents, family, just a normal, regular childhood. (Hutson and Liddiard 1991b:24)

In Wales, as elsewhere, homeless youth have a variety of living options that include a private flat or bedsit (room), staying with friends, sleeping rough (outside), and squatting (living in an unoccupied place). Hutson and Liddiard found what they termed "homeless careers," a pattern of accommodation dependent on the length of time a youth had been homeless. Table 4.1 summarizes the experiences of different youths. It is clear that staying with friends constitutes a clear option at the beginning of one's homelessness, but becomes less probable as the months and years go by. On the other hand, sleeping rough becomes more frequent in the more advanced stages of the homeless career. It is also interesting to note that somewhere near the initial stages, the young person tries to return home, although the attempt is usually short lived.

Gay, age 24, describes some of the problems associated with two of the types of accommodations that she had tried—renting from the private sector (private bedsits and flats) and sleeping rough:

Victorian slum, it was like that! Small, tiny little room. . . . We nearly got killed in there because we had a fire, a big fire, because he [the landlord] tried to put the electrics in himself. We all ended up in hospital! . . . He's a filthy old sod too. He'd get fresh with you—I ended up putting a padlock on my door. (Hutson and Liddiard 1991b:29)

[In reply to a question about the hardest thing about sleeping rough:]

Not being able to have a wash and clean clothes, going without food, getting attacked and things like that. . . . I mean, I got raped. . . . (Hutson and Liddiard 1991b:35)

Images of Street Children

Homeless children tend to gravitate to other children in an attempt to gain the nurturing and support from one another that is ideally provided by the family. However, these bonds cannot erase the street child's vulnerability to violence and exploitation at the hands of adults. One of the most powerful ways people learn about homeless children is through film. Three excellent fictionalized accounts of street children in recent years are *Pixote* (1981, director: Hector Babenco), *Salaam Bombay* (1986, director: Mira Nair), and *My Sky, My Home* (1990, director: Eros Djarot). Set in São Paulo, Brazil, Bombay, India, and Jakarta, Indonesia, each shows a different facet of life on the streets for children trying to survive on their own.

The most brutal of the three films, *Pixote*, begins with the life of children confined to a jail-like institution for abandoned children accused of crimes. The victimization and constant intimidation of the children through gang rape, beatings, and murder, and the complicity and cover-up of the institution staff, are the nightmarish result of locking up children in understaffed, corrupt institutions. When a group of children (including the hero of the film, a boy of about 11 named Pixote) escapes from the institution, life on the streets is little better. Survival involves picking pockets, drug dealing, and pimping for a prostitute. The crimes escalate to the boys committing murder. The inescapable conclusion is that the victimized quickly become victimizer, and there are no nonexploitive adults to save the children. Fernando Da Silva, the child star of the film and himself a street child when he met the director, was killed by the police in 1987 during a store robbery (CHILDHOPE 1987).

A less violent but equally sad portrayal of street children is presented by *Salaam Bombay*. In the film, Krishna, a child of about 10, runs away from his family and his village because of an accusation that he stole a bicycle, as well as the fact that his family is extremely poor and cannot support him. Arriving in Bombay for what he thinks will be a short stay and hoping to make enough money to take the train back to his village (the location of which he does not know), he becomes involved with other street children, drug addicts, and prostitutes. As the film progresses and Krishna becomes more entrenched in life on the streets, he becomes known as Chaipu (tea, bread), a name that refers to his job of carrying tea for a street vendor. Finally, Chaipu gets picked up by the authorities, who place him in a large, anonymous, overcrowded orphanage. In the last scene of the film, he has run away from the monotony and violence of the institution to seek independence on the streets once again. His dream of returning to his village and family grows dimmer and dimmer as survival becomes paramount.

In *My Sky, My Home* director Eros Djarot presents us with Gempol,

Little girls, with doll.

UNICEF/Claudio Edinger.

a child living with his family in a *kampung* (squatter settlement) by the side of railroad tracks in Jakarta, Indonesia. The implication is that the family has recently migrated from their village in rural Indonesia to the city. The boy, who helps his family survive by collecting newspapers and reselling them as trash, is accused of stealing when he is found peeking into a classroom of upper-class children. One of the boys in the classroom, Andrei, a disaffected upper-class child, who lives with his inattentive father (Andrei's mother has died) and whose major source of affection is provided by his family's servants, witnesses the commotion and contrives to meet Gempol.

Eventually, the boys become friends. When Gempol's shack is destroyed by government officials in preparation for Independence Day celebrations (and, therefore, foreign visitors), he and Andrei, who by now has the nickname Brother Small, go to the countryside to find Gempol's extended family. In their week away from Jakarta, Brother Small learns to survive in the informal economy—washing dishes for a tea stall and serving as a "parking boy" in a gang of street children. One night Gempol and Brother Small are robbed. Although their vulnerability in sleeping outside without adult protection is underscored in their encounter with the thief, the viewer breathes a sigh of relief that worse has not happened.

This film, unlike *Salaam Bombay* and *Pixote*, ends on a note of optimism—Gempol eventually returns to his village with the hope of attending school, and Brother Small returns to his family with a "raised consciousness" about the issues of poverty and inequality in his society. It is left to be seen whether his weeks on the streets will eventually be translated into action in adult life.

Violence toward Street Children

Homeless children, especially those visible on the street, are vulnerable to violence. Amnesty International has reported beatings, torture, and killings of street children in Guatemala City and in various cities in Brazil. There were press reports of 624 violent killings of children in fifteen Brazilian states during the eighteen months leading up to July 1989. In 130 of the cases the killings were attributed to death squads, which police authorities in Rio de Janeiro, Recife, and Manau have acknowledged included many off-duty police (Amnesty International 1990).

In one example of a child believed to be killed by a death squad, the body of Patricio Hilario da Silva, aged nine, was found dumped in the suburb of Ipanema on May 22, 1989. A note tied around his neck read: "I killed you because you didn't study and had no future. . . . The government must not allow the streets of the city to be invaded by kids" (Amnesty International 1990:3).

Sanders reports that a significant number of street children in Rio have been picked up by the police not for an infraction, but for simply being on the street (1987:3). Further, they are at times harassed, have the material that they sell confiscated, and are pressured for bribes (Sanders 1987:6). In Colombia, youth who are picked up by the police and/or institutionalized are forced to have their heads shaved in order to make identification easier (Felsman 1981:42; Aptekar 1988:221).

Survival Strategies

Children survive on the streets by working in the informal economy, begging, and through "survival sex."

Working

It is difficult to distinguish between homeless children who work on the street and children who work alongside their parents (Barker and Knaul 1991). The jobs of street children require few skills, offer little training, and may be dangerous and injurious to their health. Typical jobs are selling cigarettes, gum, candy, or newspapers; hauling garbage; guarding cars; washing windshields; and carrying luggage. Children who haul and scavenge for garbage often suffer cuts from shards of glass and metal. Further, street children are victims of unscrupulous adults who may abuse them, steal their earnings, or refuse to pay them. The money earned in a day is immediately spent on food, shelter, and recreation, or is given to the child's family (Barker and Knaul 1991:8).

There are an estimated 52 million children working throughout the world (International Labour Office 1980). A percentage of these children are bonded labor, wherein the labor of an entire family, including children, is used to repay the interest on a loan, while the principal of the loan remains unpaid for years or generations (Shah 1987:75).

Begging

Although begging is mentioned as a survival strategy in many reports on street children, there are few systematic studies of the practice. One exception is a study of beggar children in Northern Nigeria, conducted from January through March 1986 by Durrenda Nash Ojanuga, then the Kaduna State Principal Social Welfare Officer. The study found that one-third of the beggars of Kaduna State were under the age of 15 (Ojanuga 1990). Fluent in Hausa and English, the study team interviewed fifty-five children in the marketplace, at the railway station, in front of the mosque, in motor parks, and along the road. A small fee was given for each interview.

Seventy-three percent of the fifty-five children were boys; 95 percent were Muslim (reflecting the dominant religion of the area); they ranged in age from 3 to 14 years, with a average age of 9.6; most were not attending school, and of the twelve who were students most (eleven) were pupils of a mallam (instructor of the Koran). Thirty percent of the children were physically disabled, but there was no evidence that any of the disabled children had been intentionally deformed. Seventy-seven percent of the children said that they were living with their parents, who were too poor or physically disabled to support them. Another 16 percent were living with Koranic scholars, and 5 percent said they lived with friends.

In London, there are reports that young homeless people are being arrested as "rogues and vagabonds" under the 1824 Vagrancy Act. The law, which was established to deal with vagrancy after the Napoleonic wars, has recently been used to fine and arrest the visibly homeless who sleep rough and beg (Carvel 1990:4).

Survival Sex

There is some documentation of survival sex among children on the street. The terms "survival sex" or "sexual exploitation" are used in place of "childhood prostitution" because they emphasize the lack of choice for children on the street (Barker and Knaul 1991).

Experiences of the Preda Human Development Center in the Philippines have shed some light on the nature of survival sex. The Center, which began in 1973 as a project for young drug abusers, first became aware of survival sex when its staff discovered venereal disease in youths 9 to 14 years old (International Catholic Child Bureau 1991). The Preda Human Development Center operates in the town of Olongapo, near the recently closed U.S. Subic Bay Naval Facility. Olongapo, known as "Gapo," has become synonymous with prostitution (Lozada n.d.).

In 1989 Preda began its Childhood for Children Center as a "residential live-in, non-institutional project" for street children and sexually exploited children. It offers alternatives to the street, helps to reconcile children with their parents, investigates and reports on activities of pedophiles, and promotes media advocacy on behalf of children.

> The children are living wild on the streets, sleeping in the parks, in their push carts in which they collect trash for a living. . . . They are offered food, new clothes, and money if they will go with tourists to a hotel or dance in a club. A syndicate of adults recruits them, makes the offer and delivers them to the customer. Others stand around known hotels where

they are picked up by the tourists and offered a good time and lots of money. Street workers find them in the garbage dump, sick and in need of first aid. . . . (International Catholic Child Bureau 1991:68–69)

A recent report from the Philippines indicates that younger and younger children are becoming involved in the sex trade because the fear of AIDS drives customers to prefer young children (Alexander 1991). Street girls are particularly vulnerable to sexually transmitted diseases, including AIDS/HIV, since they frequently do not have the power to convince their sex partners to use condoms (Barker 1991b).

Whether children on the street are surviving by working, begging, or sex, they are not in school. Their time on the streets fails to prepare them as self-sufficient members of society, with a skill to offer, and they do not have the protection of adults to prevent their own exploitation.

Health Issues

Homeless children experience serious health problems. A child who is trying to survive on the street may not have access to clean water, sanitary facilities, adequate nutrition, and rest. In addition, there are specific health hazards related to various kinds of jobs. In discussing health risks and children's work, Shah (1987) emphasizes some of the many risks that a child must face.

The working sites may be full with lead fumes, dust, particles of silica, asbestos, lead or other metals and cotton fibers. In sari embroidery factories and carpet weaving industries, children sit in insufficiently lit rooms and a flexed position for long hours while working. In Sivakashi, India 52,000 children presently work in match and fireworks factories. These children are brought to the factories in buses from villages as far as 30 km away between three and five o'clock every morning and they are dropped back to their villages between six and nine o'clock in the evening after having contributed a 12-hour day's work without any intermission or rest period [Bannerjee 1979, as cited in Shah 1987:74]. Similarly, in . . . Thailand, some of the child laborers working in dingy little factories were allowed to come out of the work place for a bath only once a month. (Bannerjee 1980, as cited in Shah 1987:74)

In the industrialized world, health problems for homeless children also are severe. Research in New York City indicates an increased rate of infant mortality among homeless women living in welfare hotels, as

Improvised shelter in São Paulo, Brazil.

UNICEF/Bill Hetzer.

compared to poor, but housed women in the same city (Chavkin et al. 1987). In the Health Care for the Homeless Program (Wright and Weber 1987) there were found to be increased rates of respiratory infections, minor skin ailments, ear disorders, gastrointestinal disorders, and infestational ailments among homeless children, when compared with the pediatric national sample. Further research reveals hunger, poor nutrition, developmental delays, and psychological problems among children living in shelters and welfare hotels (Rafferty and Shinn 1991).

In Toronto, research of the Department of Paediatrics at the University of Toronto on the health of the city's street children indicated that most (75 percent) were under 15 years old, most had dropped out of school before turning 14, and most (87 percent) were drug abusers (Goldman 1988:1041). Many of the youths were malnourished.

Although the girls in the study were sexually active, many thought that they would not contract a sexually transmitted disease. In fact, almost 50 percent of the girls had chlamydia. An important issue for health practitioners from the Toronto study is how few of the youth told their doctors about their life-style.

Another obvious health issue is the risk of HIV/AIDS among homeless children. In a conference in San Francisco in June 1990, representatives of thirty-two countries met for the International Conference on Homeless Youth and AIDS. The few studies that had been conducted prior to this date had found a seroprevalence rate of 2 to 10 percent among street children (Barker and Knaul 1990). In addition to the health risks is the stigmatizing of street children due to fear of AIDS. For example, Dr. Gloria Ornelas Hall, of the Centro de Información Nacional in Mexico, concluded:

> AIDS is stigmatizing street children worldwide. In some countries . . . there has been a reluctance to discuss AIDS or carry out testing to detect the incidence of the disease for fear of discrimination or repression against street youth. In Colombia and Brazil, for example, vigilante groups have killed street children because they are suspected of being carriers of AIDS. One Mexican street youth was put in prison and held in total isolation when he tested HIV-positive; guards fed him by sliding his food under the door. (Barker and Knaul 1990:1)

Among the strategies recommended to reach youth on the street that emerged from the conference was recruiting former and current prostitutes as peer educators to reach girls on the street regarding AIDS. Abstinence as a strategy was thought to be unrealistic.

Glue Sniffing

Another health risk associated with street youth is the sniffing of glue and other inhalants (Justin 1987). Street youths (especially boys) inhale glue by spreading it on a rag or putting it in a plastic bag, putting the rag or plastic bag over their nose, and inhaling. The inhalants produce a sense of euphoria and distort shape, color, time, and sound. Sniffing inhalants also can lead to a loss of inhibitions and to violent behavior.

The damaging effects of glue inhalation include nausea, excess salivation, and vomiting, with occasional aspiration of the vomitus, which can lead to pneumonia or death. There may be kidney and liver damage, severe electrolyte disturbance, and central nervous system problems such as seizure and encephalitis. The substances used to mix the inhalants, such as cleaning fluid, also are dangerous, possibly causing liver and bone marrow damage.

One suggestion put forth to stop glue sniffing is to have glue manufacturers add noxious smells to the glue in an effort to dissuade the user (Justin 1987). The use of mustard oil, for example, would cause a burning sensation similar to that produced by eating horseradish.

Programs and Policies for Homeless Children

The growing concern for street children has produced a growing body of recommendations for dealing with their problems. Fabio Dallape, director of the Undugu Society of Kenya, has developed some guidelines for working with street children, using his experience in Nairobi (1991). His guidelines recommend that the individual (1) start out by talking casually with the children on the street and be prepared for a give and take because the children will also be curious about the adult; (2) pay market price (not more) if the child does something for you; (3) begin by helping the children with something they can use right away— a new game or ways to improve their business; (4) be very cautious about adopting the child, because it is difficult to absorb a child into one's life permanently; (5) not be too quick to pay the child's school expenses, because one cannot be sure if the child really wants to go to school and whether he will be successful; and (6) realize that surveys are not a good first contact—many students, researchers, and police have already questioned the children, often without positive results.

One type of person working with homeless children is the "street educator." According to the agency CHILDHOPE, street education refers to both the site of education (the street) and the methodology of informal education. The street educator respects the values of the child and educates him or her through example and interest. An example of a street school is the Nukkad (street corner) Center, a school for street children in Bombay, India, that was created by Mira Nair through funds from the proceeds of *Salaam Bombay* (Crossette 1990). The center offers informal education to approximately thirty boys ages 5 to 16 who live at the New Delhi railroad station.

There are many complicated issues involved with working with girls on the street. Young women may have been or are still in danger of being sexually exploited. In many societies, those who are sexually active are considered de facto adults. Girls involved in prostitution are severely condemned, and those who do not want to prostitute themselves are at a disadvantage because there are fewer alternative work situations for girls than for boys. Furthermore, girls on the street are not well thought of even by the agencies and organizations working with street children (Ward 1987).

One innovative though macabre approach to addressing the violence perpetrated against street children is the Brazilian CHILDHOPE program called PROJICA. The objective is to humanize the death of a street child by finding him "adoptive" parents who are able to provide a proper burial. The "parents" give the dead child their last name (Barker 1991a). PROJICA is also establishing support networks of religious, legal, and civic organizations to protect children against violence from police and vigilante groups.

Common sleeping conditions in the Copacabana, Rio de Janiero, Brazil.

UNICEF/Bill Hetzer

It is clear that although we know more about homeless children than about either homeless men or women in various parts of the world, the very concept of "homeless children" varies from one culture to another. In developing countries, the focus has been on street children, the most visible and "problematic" of the group. However, unknown numbers of other children live in various kinds of orphanages and institutions, hidden from public view. In the United States, the term "homeless children" most often refers to children in homeless shelters and welfare hotels, while children staying with their family in a "doubled-up" situation are hidden from view. In Eastern Europe, the term most often refers to children who have been abandoned and are living in institutions.

Street children, deprived of the care and protection of adults, are left to survive on their own, using any means possible. Children who live in shelters and welfare hotels are subject to the lack of privacy and humiliating and at times unsafe conditions. Children in institutions face authoritarianism and isolation. There is a sense of urgency about the problem of homeless children that challenges the creativity and resourcefulness of the rest of society.

5
Homeless Families

[New York, New York] When Marisol LaFontaine left the city's homeless shelter system after two months in 1990, it was not because she had found a place of her own. Not even close.

She left on the spur of the moment when she saw the latest hotel she and her three children had been sent to, a decrepit building in Harlem where people smoked crack openly at the front door. Even the manager encouraged her to move. . . .

Ms. LaFontaine, who said she became homeless when the pharmacy where she worked closed and she could not find another job, took her children from the Harlem hotel to live with a friend in her old neighborhood in Morrisania, the Bronx. But that friend had a three-room apartment and four children of her own, and the arrangement collapsed after about a month. And back the LaFontaines went to the hotels. (Bennet 1992)

[Bombay, India] Many pavement dwellers get their water supply from municipal fire hydrants. These are opened during the night and the requisite water is piped off. Men usually take baths in groups near the hydrant itself. As one investigator described it, a man takes his bath on an installment basis. That is to say, he stands in the queue, moves towards the tap and washes his body. He then comes out to the footpath and applies soap. Again he has to wait in the serpentine queue to wash away the soap.

Most families do not possess cots. Some have only one huge mattress made up of torn clothes. The whole family sleeps on it. Some have only one bed which is used by the head of the household. Some tie their bed sheets to their legs with string to prevent theft of the sheets when they are asleep. (Ramchandaran 1972:31)

It is in reference to homeless families that in world perspective, the word *homelessness* takes on the greatest variety of meanings. It is also here that the two words, "homeless" and "families," present us with a paradox and with a departure from the more classic concept of homelessness as a "detachment from society" (Caplow, Bahr, and Sternberg 1968). The very act of being a family is an affirmation of the ability to bond, despite the hardships of inadequate or lack of shelter.

For our purposes, a family is defined as "a social and economic unit consisting minimally of a parent and children" (Ember and Ember 1990:511). This generic definition accommodates the great variety of family structures found throughout the world: the nuclear family (two parents and child/children); the one-parent family; the extended family (three or more generations in one household, usually linked by parental ties, but sometimes linked by sibling ties); the polygynous family (one man, multiple wives, with the relationship of co-wives in the household); and the polyandrous family (one woman, multiple husbands).

In world perspective, homeless families include families in homeless shelters and welfare hotels, pavement dwellers, and families in squatter settlements. The common dilemma facing all homeless families is the inadequacy of shelter and its tenuous nature. Among the strategies for survival used by homeless families are doubling up with family and friends; living in abandoned cars, empty houses, out-of-the-way parks, campgrounds, and chicken coops (all hidden from view); seeking shelter in battered women's homes (if the women and children leave home because of abuse), which are not counted as homeless shelters even though the women and children cannot find other housing; splitting up the family (children move in with relatives); and placing the children voluntarily in foster care, rather than making them face life in a shelter or welfare hotel.

Homeless families have an invisibility about them similar to that experienced by homeless women. First, they do not conform to the classic image of the male hobo. Second, at least in North America and in Western Europe, homeless families may be in hiding, due to the not totally misplaced anxiety that to present oneself to the "authorities" as a homeless family means risking the loss of the children to foster care (see Pearce 1988).

Historical Perspectives

Despite the popular impression that homelessness among families, at least in the industrialized world, is a new phenomenon, homeless families have existed for some time. Two examples are the *chiffonniers* (ragpickers) of Paris and the "automobile families" of the United States.

Les Chiffonniers

> In the bosom of the Capital lives a large class of individuals whose lot seems to be poverty: the rag pickers, a kind of nomad population, which has gotten much bigger these last years, foreign to all social habits, obeying no rule, knowing no restraint, accustomed to an almost wild independence, constantly roaming all over Paris . . . believing to have acquired the right, by dint of long enjoyment of it, to explore the public rights of way, at all hours of day or night, without any guarantee, without a fixed domicile, sometimes even without shelter, isolated in a way from the large family (of man), walking, armed with an instrument [the steel hooks they use to pick up the rags] which, innocent in its purpose, could in perverse hands, become the instrument of crime; these unhappy folk are the object of worry for peaceful folk. (Prefect of Police, Debelleyme, Paris, September 1828, as cited in Kalff 1990:19–20)

Ragpickers lived on the periphery of Paris from the fourteenth century. Made up of men, women, and children, they gathered the rubbish the people of Paris would pile up on the streets each nightfall and lived in any available hut they could find. Several notables of Paris wandered into the ragpickers' living area in 1831, during a cholera epidemic:

> In these stinking, dark holes, indescribably unhealthy, the notables were surely fearful of source of infection. But what seemed to trouble them deeply was the way of life of these inhabitants. In their accounts, the rag pickers evoked pictures of a kind of hell, pictures of men and women lying pell-mell on the ground among animals and unspeakable debris, from which came the foulest odors. (Kalff 1990:21)

A forced exodus of Paris's ragpickers took place between 1850 and 1860, when the "Haussmanization" of the city was accomplished. Baron Haussman was responsible for the creation of the broad boulevards of Paris and the razing of older buildings along them. At various times in their history the ragpickers were able to organize and advocate for themselves, and at other times they were forced to move farther and farther away from the city, the site of their economic survival.

Automobile Families

In the United States during the 1920s, there could be found "automobile families," who would arrive in town by auto, pitch camp in any available spot, and then apply to welfare agencies for support (Gilmore 1940). By the time the welfare investigation was complete, they had left town to begin the process somewhere else. Some automobile families were in fact migratory workers in either agriculture or construction.

Descriptions of Homeless Families

North America and Western Europe

The shortage of affordable and appropriate housing in the urban centers of North America and Western Europe has often been attributed to the transformation of cities from manufacturing to service-based economies (these cities are often referred to as postindustrial). In this transformation, low-rent housing is demolished and replaced by offices, retail complexes, and luxury high-rise apartments. In addition, large numbers of old and deteriorated units stand vacant, ready to be demolished or renovated. The housing "shortage" may more properly be called a housing "maladjustment" in that there are theoretically enough units for the urban population, but the units are not affordable to many of the people who need them most (Adams 1986:527).

   A label for this loss of affordable housing is *gentrification*, a term attributed to Ruth Glass (1964), who described the process whereby the "gentry" of Britain began to buy up and renovate old buildings in the 1960s. Gentrification is now widely used, despite the fact that the British "gentry" have nothing to do with this process in London or the rest of the world. Although gentrification is for the most part used with reference to the industrialized world, it may also describe similar processes in parts of the developing world. For example, gentrification can be seen in the renovation of the old port area (now the "upscale" Redcliffe Quay) of St. John's, Antigua, and the subsequent loss of space by and restriction of access for black Antiguans (Thomas 1991).

In Western Europe, one finds reference to the "new homeless," those people whose lack of housing is not due to the post–World War II housing crisis (1940s and 1950s) but to contemporary housing conditions. When "new homeless" is used in the United States, it tends to refer to homeless families, in contrast to the "traditional" skid row populations.

England

Perhaps no nation in Western Europe has focused so much attention on homelessness as England, which has numerous advocacy groups and research foundations devoted to the problem. Under the Housing (Homeless Persons) Act of 1977, England considers someone to be homeless:

> if there is no accommodation which he and anyone who normally resides with him as a member of his family or anyone the housing authority consider is reasonable to reside with him . . .; or if he has accommodation but cannot secure entry to it, or if it is probable that his occupation of it will lead to either violence or real threats of violence from someone else residing there. The Act defines categories of homeless people who are considered to be in "priority need" for accommodation. The first and foremost category of the "priority need" household are those who have responsibility for dependent children. Single homeless people are only considered to be in priority need if they are "vulnerable as a result of old age, mental illness and handicap, or physical disability or other special reasons." (Housing (Homeless Person) Act S.2(1)(c), as cited in Watson and Austerberry 1986:11–12)

Excluded from the definition of the homeless are those whom the housing authority can prove to be "intentionally" homeless.

This definition guides local authorities in deciding who will get council (public) housing and how soon. The discretionary term "unintentional" has been used by some local authorities to eliminate families who have become homeless through an inability to pay rent arrears. In some places higher priority for housing is given to people from the local area (sometimes meaning those who have lived in a place from two to five years). The "local connection" serves as a way to screen out recent migrants and immigrants to London (Adams 1986).

At times, the numbers of homeless in England have been estimated by using the numbers of people accepted as homeless by the official definition and those on the waiting lists for council housing. This excludes people who are not accepted as homeless, as well as those who have never applied for assistance.

An unforeseen effect of defining a family as "homeless" using the council housing authority method is that if a homeless family rejects housing offered by the council, it can be categorized as "intentionally" homeless (Murie and Forrest 1988).

> Hackney (council housing) offered me a place—but I refused it. They said it was the last offer I would get. It was filthy, no heating, a basement flat, plaster falling off the walls, dark and damp. It only had two rooms— no room for the kids. A shared bathroom and toilet. The council said I could put the kids in the sitting-room. It was hopeless. They were trying to dump me off with anything. I would have been really stuck. I knew no one in the area. (Watson and Austerberry 1986:119)

There is a great variety of temporary accommodations for families in England, which include hostels (shelters), bed and breakfast hotels (similar to welfare hotels in the United States), and the temporary leasing of private and public housing. During 1989 and 1990 there were an estimated 200,000 families in England and Wales living in temporary accommodations, and that figure is expected to rise to 500,000 by 1995 (Joseph Rowntree Foundation 1991). But the distinction between "temporary" and "permanent" accommodation becomes blurred when families are forced to stay in emergency accommodations for several years. In addition, families may be forced to share accommodations, which is known as "hidden" or "concealed" homelessness.

Conditions in bed and breakfast hotels are similar to those in welfare hotels in the United States:

> For families, cramped space, lack of privacy and absence of playspace is severe. While lack of privacy is most likely to be expressed by adults, children's awareness of their housing situation is evident in expressions about their lack of a home. All of these factors contribute to behavioural and psychological problems and to increasing stress in the family. These

problems are made worse the longer the time spent in such accommodation. (Murie and Forrest 1988:140–141)

Germany

In Germany, there has been a significant rise in the number of homeless families (*Der Spiegel* 1992). In the major cities of Germany, some people live in subway tunnels, under bridges, in underground garages, and in car and tent cities. The Housing Department of Cologne estimates that 45,000 people (five percent of the city's population) now live in communal emergency quarters. Affordable apartments in the urban centers of Germany are extremely rare. A working father of three, with a net monthly income .of 1,800 marks (approximately U.S. $1,170), laments: "to find an apartment in the private sector is as unattainable to me as becoming a millionaire" (*Der Spiegel* 1992:76).

In Germany, the mayors of each city are responsible for housing the homeless. The seemingly cheapest solution is to build container villages (prefabricated housing) or place the homeless in rooming houses, rather than assume their rental debts. For example:

> Heinz Dirkes, 46, [is in] a homeless shelter in Berlin. Officials stuck him, his wife and four children into three small rooms of 37 square meters having to share the kitchen with six other parties.
>
> A year and a half earlier the Dirkeses had had a 100 square meter apartment. But when the tool maker became unemployed he quickly got behind with his rent. They were evicted.

In Cologne, the Department of Housing Assistance takes over rents in emergency situations, rather than placing people in ghetto-like container villages or shelters. Each year, approximately 12,000 cases of imminent homelessness are handled, with an average cost of 1,000 marks per case—a marked improvement over the 8,000 marks it costs for each new shelter resident. However, subsidizing rents cannot make up for the lack of affordable units. Approximately 5 million apartments would have to be built by the year 2000 in order to house the German population. Affordable apartments are lost each day due to condo conversions, modernization, and commercial use. As has been noted in England, Germany is experiencing a growing gap between rich and poor, with homelessness the symbol of poverty.

France

In France, in the early part of the twentieth century before the construction of public housing, one in four people lived in half a room, and tuberculosis was rampant. The housing situation inspired Le Corbusier, the famous French architect (1887–1965), to exclaim: "Cannons? Munitions? No, thank you, housing please!" (Ferrand-Bechmann 1990:76).

It is estimated that in 1986 there were between 200,000 and 400,000 people in emergency lodging in France (Wresinski 1987; Ferrand-Bechmann 1988:147). This figure does not include the squatters living in vacant housing or those doubled-up with other families. The homeless in France include the same mix as elsewhere in Western Europe: young single people, men, women, and families.

In a review of the social organizations providing shelter for the homeless, Professor Dan Ferrand-Bechmann of the Université de Grenoble documents the work of a variety of nongovernmental agencies active in France that focus on the needs of the homeless. Among them are the Salvation Army, which offers shelters for the homeless and pays the rents of homeless families in hotels; the Quart Monde (Fourth World), which helps people pay their rent and is active politically (the staff of Quart Monde also lives in the neighborhoods with the people); Emmaus, an organization begun by l'Abbé Pierre that funds soup kitchens and shelters under its own auspices (l'Abbé Pierre also organized a social housing program for homeless people and began an industry of recycling and fixing old furniture, electric equipment, and clothes); and the Fédération Nationale des Associations d'Accueil et de Réadaptation Sociale (FNARS), a large network of organizations whose main task is housing the homeless. There are also many religiously affiliated organizations, such as the Fédération Nationale de l'Entraide Protestante, a Protestant agency that pays for hotels and offers shelter; Fonds Social Juif Unifié, a Jewish organization based primarily in Paris and Marseilles that helps the homeless financially; Les Petits Frères des Pauvres, a Catholic agency working mostly with the elderly; Le Secours Catholique, a Catholic agency sheltering homeless single people and families; La Société Saint-Vincent de Paul, which shelters the homeless; the Red Cross, which runs emergency shelters; and L'Union des Foyers de Jeunes Travailleurs, originally offering lodging to young workers, but more recently including young people who cannot pay their rent (Ferrand-Bechmann 1988).

An interesting generic term used in France for shelters and reception centers is "centres de réinsertion sociale" (centers for social reentry or reinsertion). This term embodies the idea that being poor and homeless puts one outside the social life of the community. It is analogous to the concept of having been "put away" in an institution (e.g., mental hospital) and needing a period of reintegration into society. It is not known how the people seeking help at the centres de réinsertion view this interpretation.

United States

In the United States, current interest in homeless families focuses on reasons for the lack of affordable housing (sometimes called the structural approach) or the characteristics of homeless families (at times criticized as "blaming the victim"). Some try to balance the structural issues related to the shortage of low-income housing and the inadequacy of Aid to Families with Dependent Children (AFDC) benefits with the breakdown of family structure (Bassuk, Rubin, and Lauriat 1986).

Contemporary interest in homeless families in the United States began with studies of families living in shelters. In 1986, eighty homeless mothers and 151 of their children were interviewed in fourteen family shelters in Massachusetts, in order to assess the reasons for their homelessness, as well as the housing, health, and psychological problems they faced (Bassuk, Rubin, and Lauriat 1986). The authors hypothesize that the most disturbed and disrupted families were not included in the sample, since these families often do not seek help from shelters or are turned away.

The interviews revealed a great deal of instability among the eighty homeless families. In the previous five years, 85 percent had been doubled-up in housing with other families, and 50 percent had lived in other emergency housing. More than 40 percent had come to the shelter from overcrowded, shared housing arrangements. Not surprisingly, a high percentage of the families evidenced psychological stress, and the children suffered from school-related problems.

One question is whether or not families would deliberately enter a shelter, thereby defining themselves as "homeless," in order to receive

preferential treatment in obtaining decent housing ("jumping" the waiting lists for public housing). In commenting on this question, Nancy
Wachstein, former director of the Office on Homelessness and Single
Room Occupancy Housing in New York City, estimated that there are
as many 200,000 ill-housed welfare families. In order to prevent them
from entering the shelter system, shelters have had to house them for
long periods of time before granting permanent housing as a way to
deter other doubled-up families from leaving their current situations in
hopes of getting apartments sooner (Dugger 1992b:9). Unfortunately,
there are indications that as many as 60 percent of the 15,000 families
who pass through the New York City shelter system each year leave
before getting any assistance in finding housing, and that many homeless families try to avoid the shelter/hotel system as long as possible
(Bennet 1992).

In addition to shelters, homeless families have been put in hotels
since the 1970s (Robbins 1986; Kozol 1988). Although the practice of
putting people in hotels (the worst of which are dangerous and degrad-
ing) has lessened in New York City since the 1970s and 1980s, by
August 1992 there were still more than 750 homeless families in welfare hotels, out of an estimated 4,750 total homeless families living in
shelters, hotels, and temporary apartments (Morgan 1992:B1).

Aside from shelters and welfare hotels, it is difficult to find temporary shelter for homeless families. For example, the Human Resources
Administration (HRA), when housing families in tourist hotels, advised
its workers *not* to inform the hotels of each family's association with
HRA, asking them to pay cash for the rooms (Morgan 1992:B1).
Although the Hotel Association objected to the duplicity involved in
hiding the family's homeless status, the HRA maintained that such
secrecy was the only way to have these families accepted. The NIMBY
(not-in-my-backyard) syndrome operates decisively in limiting residential options for homeless families.

The unrest facing many homeless families is indicated by the life of
Josephine Carter, a 38-year-old woman with five children ranging in
age from 4 to 15.

> Josephine Carter closed the door behind herself and her five children for
> the last time on December 27, 1983. Behind her she left a one-family
> house on a leafy street in Cambria Heights in southeastern Queens. Once
> the property of her common-law husband, they had lived in the home for

ten years until they separated and the bank foreclosed on a mortgage she could no longer pay.

As she and her children came down the stoop they stepped across this city's sharpest dividing line between haves and have-nots, between the merely poor and the desperate. They stepped out of one world and into another. They were now homeless.

At her Income Maintenance Center she was told to get, as best she could, to Roberto Clemente State Park, a gymnasium in the The Bronx that had been made over into a mass shelter for families by the city.

"I looked down into the place," recalled Carter, "and saw all those little cots and all those people. There were these state troopers walking around on the balcony, and the guards down below. I couldn't believe it. The kids said, 'I feel like I'm in prison, but I didn't do nothing wrong.'" (Robbins 1986:26–27)

After leaving the Roberto Clemente shelter, the Carter family was placed in the Hotel Carter in Times Square, where the city paid $95 per night for a ten-foot by twelve-foot room with one bed, a cot, and moldy fungus crawling across the bathroom ceiling. The hotel charged any guest (including baby sitters) $12.50 just to go upstairs. The Carter family stayed there for eight months, after which they were moved because Josephine Carter was harassed by the hotel guards for speaking at a rally. She and her family were then placed in another hotel. During their time at the Hotel Carter, management refused to comply with city orders to provide window guards or air conditioners to prevent children from falling out of the windows. Instead, management chained the windows shut in a number of rooms—mothers had to smash them open to let in fresh air (Robbins 1986:32).

Our knowledge of homeless families in the United States has been enhanced by comparisons with poor, but housed families. In a study of social relationships (Shinn, Knickman, and Weitzman 1991), 677 homeless mothers and 495 poor but housed mothers were interviewed in English and Spanish in New York City. The homeless families were interviewed upon their request for shelter at the Emergency Assistance Unit, the access point for both public and nonprofit family shelters in New York City. A strong feature of this research was that families were interviewed *before* entering a shelter, so that characteristics developed by residence in a shelter would not be confused with characteristics of the families themselves. Current social relationships (number of contacts, the ability to stay with them, and availability of help) as well as childhood social relationships were explored. The social network in the study included friends and relatives. A surprising finding was that the *homeless* respondents maintained closer ties with their social networks than their housed counterparts but at the same time were less able to stay with relatives and friends—in large part because they had already "worn out their welcome" by staying with them during the previous year.

In a study of the prevalence of abuse and violence (Goodman 1991), fifty homeless and fifty housed AFDC mothers were interviewed extensively regarding current and past abuse. Physical violence and sexual abuse were determined by using standard measures covering both childhood and adulthood experience. There were no significant differences between the homeless and the housed samples. In fact, both the homeless and the housed respondents reported extraordinarily high prevalence rates of abuse: 90 percent of the homeless sample and 88 percent of the housed sample had endured some form of physical or sexual abuse during their lifetimes (Goodman 1991:497).

Eastern Europe

> As evening falls, dozens of people, including families with children and grandparents, make themselves at home on blankets and cardboard along the corridors of the Keleti train station, hanging out damp towels, opening tins of canned food, getting into position for the night ahead. (Bohlen 1990:A1)

In Hungary, an estimated 20,000 people are homeless (Bohlen 1990). Homelessness is thought to be in part a by-product of the move from communism to the market economy. Under communism, sleeping in parks and in public and begging were considered crimes of "parasitism," punishable by imprisonment. All persons had to be registered at an address. Now, however, a person can be expelled by a hostile relative; factories have closed hostels housing several thousand single men; and 3,000 prisoners were freed in June 1990. A chronic housing shortage and large number of alcoholics and drifters (which predate the political changes) coupled with these new developments have created a problem of homelessness for which Hungarian society appears unprepared. In October 1990, the city of Budapest maintained only 1,500 shelter beds and had a capacity to provide 300 meals a day. It is estimated that approximately half of the homeless in Hungary are Romanians who have come to Hungary because of a loosening of travel restrictions in their country.

The Developing World

Much of the interest in "homelessness" in the developing world focuses on the hundreds of thousands of people living in informal or squatter settlements. However, some of the research on the developing world includes families outside of squatter communities, as examples from China and India demonstrate.

Rural-to-Urban Migrants in China

In China, the *mong liu*, "blindly migrating people," most closely approximate our conception of homeless families (Ye Qimao 1992). Another term, *nong min gong*, refers specifically to peasants who come to the city to work (Guo 1992). Both terms refer to a rural-to-urban migration without official governmental approval. Initially, migrants have no place to live, and therefore at least some spend their nights sleeping in railroad stations, harbors, and empty buildings. Because they come to the city without registering, they are not counted in the national census and contribute to an underestimate of China's urban population (Ye Qimao 1992).

In the late 1980s, great numbers of *mong liu* moved from the countryside to the cities due to the closing of rural industries, the suspension of large-scale construction projects, and a reduced demand for field workers. It is estimated that there were as many as 100 million "blind migrants," who together formed a floating population, unattached to any collectivity and, in theory, illegal. Despite less education and fewer skills than their city-born contemporaries, these blind migrants have great initiative and have become the self-employed peddlers, cobblers, repairmen, and tailors of the cities (Pye 1991:463).

Pavement Dwellers of India

Life for a street family demands a highly efficient use of space and a reliance on only the essentials for survival. In Bombay, families construct "dwellings" using the side of a building as a backwall and a tarpaulin supported by bamboo poles as a roof. The entire place is generally six feet by four feet and can be dismantled within ten minutes if there is a raid (Ramchandaran 1972). Inside the small area

> the iron trunks containing valuable household items are usually kept safely against the back wall only. . . . The location of the kitchen cooking place is dependent on available space. It is sometimes inside but more often outside, and adjacent to the dwelling. . . . These dwellings have no doors, but the entrances are covered with sarees. When the woman takes her bath, she has another member of the household at the entrance of the dwelling as a watch. (Ramchandaran 1972:30)

In Calcutta, the majority of the pavement dwellers have migrated from the rural areas of West Bengal or Bangladesh, because they could not support themselves in their villages. On the road, the families camp on any available pavement or canal bank or in any park or railway station (Das 1986:96). They thus have become known as *footpath basti*, the word *basti* referring to their tarpaulin-covered shelter. Generations of footpath *basti* are born with no hope of returning to life in the village, eventually losing all contact with their kin. Once in the city, they become porters, day laborers, handcart-pullers, ragpickers, and mason's helpers, and some of them beggars, pickpockets, or prostitutes (Das 1986). Social life on the pavement is very different from social life in the village, especially in terms of the disintegration of relationships among kin outside of the immediate household and the growing independence and individualism of household members.

> In most of the cases the family organisation is so loosely arranged that the members have the liberty to do anything they like. The relationship between husband and wife is unstable. The husbands whose wives work outside and contribute sufficient amount for maintaining the family, admit that their wives no longer oblige them by obeying whatever they say regarding domestic matters. So also is the behaviour of the earning of [*Sic*] sons and daughters. . . . The behavioural pattern between husband and wife, *vasur* [husband's elder brother] and younger brother's wife or uncle and nephew, etc. reveals that in all cases the elements of respect seem to be lacking and the social distance has been shortened considerably. Smoking *bidi* [inexpensive cigarettes] or hemp or cutting jokes with elderly persons have become common. (Das n.d.:302)

Survival Strategies

Squatting refers to building either a shelter of easily found materials on property to which one has no legal claim or to moving into an abandoned building or shelter. Although initially it was almost exclusively a phenomenon of the developing world, squatting is now recognized as a survival strategy in the industrialized world.

Squatting in the Developing World

The literature on the world's squatter settlements is vast. The name most closely associated with research and advocacy regarding squatter settlements is John Turner whose book *Housing by People: Towards Autonomy in Building Environments* (1976) was the seminal presentation of the potential of squatter settlements. Initially, squatter settlements were seen as temporary, makeshift arrangements for new but "unintegrated" rural migrants to urban areas. Words associated with the settlements were social breakdown, marginality (often implying physical, social, and economic marginality), public eyesore, and "urban cancer." By the late 1960s, however, squatter settlements were being seen as rational alternatives to the housing shortage for low-income people (Moser 1987). Often, they were called self-help housing, spontaneous settlements, or, in Peru, young towns (*pueblos jóvenes*). Governments shifted from demolishing the settlements to encouraging them through sites and services projects (making available new plots of land with water connections, electricity, and sanitation), and squatter upgrading projects. Critics of governmental encouragement of self-help point out that it absolves governments from committing significant amounts of money to housing projects, and that it also reduces the wage requirements of workers by giving them access to low-cost housing.

A classic route to the squatter settlement is through migration from the countryside to the city. Originally, the family rents a single room. Because the room is too expensive, the family eventually invades waste land and builds squatter housing out of abandoned local material that they find. The settlement is often repeatedly burned down, through official acts of squatter clearance, as well as accidents.

The Undugu (Brotherhood) Society in Nairobi, Kenya, is an example of a nongovernmental community organization that provides shantytown dwellers with access to land and permission to build dwellings out of purchased or scavenged materials. Typical of a person helped by such a project is Monica Wanjiru, who was born and raised in a farming area of the Rift Valley in Kenya. She completed grade three of primary school in the late 1930s before dropping out to take care of her siblings. At age 16, she married a farmer who died during the fight for independence. Monica then moved with her four children to Nairobi, where they lived in a single room (with an outside kitchen and a common toilet shared by seven households), their rent paid for by the Bahati Community Center. She herself earned money at the community center by weaving traditional banana fiber baskets for the tourist market and by selling vegetables among her neighbors. By 1969, however, the community centre stopped paying rents in Bahati. As several of her (now) eight children had to pay school fees, Monica could no longer afford the monthly rent of the single room.

> By 1969 she and her large household joined other squatters on waste land at the bottom of Bahati hill, right on the banks of the ever more polluted Nairobi River. Monica, with the help of her sons and daughters, quickly erected a single room shanty made out of packing cases and cardboard as well as mud and wattle. . . .
>
> Between the years 1969 and 1984, when she was living in her crate and cardboard shanty, Monica's home was repeatedly burned down, several times by the staff of the city council who engaged in extensive squatter clearance operations between the years 1970 and 1975. At other times, her shanty, which was built wall to wall with her neighbors, burned when cooking or beer brewing fires broke out and quickly spread from one house to another. . . .
>
> Monica's present optimism seems to date from a time in 1984 when social workers from the Undugu (Brotherhood) Society of Kenya set up an office and began surveying as well as organizing their Kanuku "village" community. These social workers had the chief's permission to resettle the squatters on the other side of the Nairobi River. . . .
>
> [S]he and her sons were allocated three very small plots around a miniature open courtyard where they could each build a two-room hut in the "New Kanuku" village. When she was shown the plots and allocated the construction materials (trees, a door, and metal roofing), Monica and her two sons set to work constructing their eighth and, hopefully, final

home in Nairobi. They had to buy tools, nails and windows for themselves aside from contributing all the labor. Soon they also hope to receive (from the Netherlands Embassy) a few bags of cement with which to permanently plaster the outside of their new homes. (UN Centre for Human Settlements 1986:201–204)

The harsh reality of living in a shantytown is portrayed by Carolina Maria De Jesus, whose first-person account of her ordeal in a Brazilian *favela, Child of the Dark: The Diary of Carolina Maria De Jesus,* was published in 1963 and has been widely read throughout the industrialized world. De Jesus herself has since died in poverty and obscurity in Brazil, little known in her own country (Levine 1992). De Jesus communicates a personal view of life and death in the favela.

Homeless refugee families in Asia.

UNHCR/Anneliese Hollmann.

Yesterday I ate that macaroni from the garbage with fear of death, because in 1953 I sold scrap over there in Zinho. There was a pretty little black boy. He also went to sell scrap in Zinho. He was young and said that those who should look for paper were the old. One day I was collecting scrap when I stopped at Bom Jardim Avenue. Someone had thrown meat into the garbage, and he was picking out the pieces. He told me:

"Take some, Carolina. It's still fit to eat."

He gave me some, and so as not to hurt his feelings, I accepted. I tried to convince him not to eat that meat, or the hard bread gnawed by the rats. He told me no, because it was two days since he had eaten. He made a fire and roasted the meat. His hunger was so great that he couldn't wait for the meat to cook. He heated it and ate. So as not to remember that scene, I left thinking, I'm going to pretend I wasn't there. This can't be real in a rich country like mine. . . .

The next day I found that little black boy dead. His toes were spread apart. The space must have [been] eight inches between them. He had blown up as if made out of rubber. His toes looked like a fan. He had no documents. He was buried like any other "Joe." (De Jesus 1963:41)

Squatting in the West

One way to survive the lack of shelter in the West is to use the "Third World" solution of squatting. Research from cities such as London, Philadelphia, Amsterdam, and Paris confirm the existence of squatters. Interestingly, these squatters are often helped by advocacy groups who fight against their eviction. For example, in London, some have noted a general (and surprising) tolerance of squatting (Adams 1986). Although in the late 1960s British authorities tried to make squatted property uninhabitable by cutting off gas and electricity, ripping up floor boards, knocking out windows, and pulling out basins, tubs, and toilets (called "municipal vandalism"), by the 1970s the authorities appeared resigned to the situation. The advocacy groups appeared to encourage working class families to squat, and the properties these families seized were primarily public housing units.

Advocacy for squatters is expressed in the *Squatters Handbook* (1987), a publication of the London-based Advisory Service for Squatters (ASS). The handbook is now in its ninth printing and gives advice on finding and entering a squat, as well as on fighting eviction.

The ASS estimates that in 1987 there were 31,000 squatters in London (1990:1).

> Squatting is not a crime. If you have heard rumours saying it has been made one, they are wrong! . . . With a few exceptions (see page 10) if you can get into an empty house or flat that nobody else is using, without doing any damage, you can make it your home. You have basically the same rights as other households: the right to privacy, rubbish collection, postal delivery, social security and essential services like water, and electricity (there can be some problems with electricity—see page 23). Many squats last only a short time, but if you choose your place carefully you may be able to stay for years. (Advisory Service for Squatters 1987:3)

In some cases, organized squatters were granted permission to occupy specific buildings, provided that their organization took the responsibility for screening tenants, managing the apartments, and vacating the building if necessary. In addition to licensing squatters, some were given the same exemption from local property taxes usually reserved for charitable organizations.

In Philadelphia, the squatter movement began during the late 1970s when a community organizer for the North Philadelphia Block Development Corporation began placing homeless families in vacant Housing and Urban Development (HUD) owned buildings. The group screened out alcoholics, drug addicts, and other high-risk people. At the same time, a nationwide advocacy group called ACORN was mobilizing families to move into city-owned property, and the city was urged to expand its own Gift Property Program. By 1982, Philadelphia's city council passed legislation for the deeding of abandoned tax-delinquent properties to squatters if they agreed to make repairs that would bring the properties up to minimum standards.

Squatting as a response to the housing shortage in the Netherlands is referred to as self-build, self-help, or shadow-housing (Turpijn 1988). Ironically, the Dutch welfare state welcomes self-help in fields such as medical services and programs for the elderly but not in housing. Nevertheless, by 1980 there were approximately 21,000 caravans and barracks, 10,000 houseboats, and 3,500 houses occupied and inhabited without permission of authorities (Turpijn 1988:108).

In addition to the individual quest for shelter, self-help housing can be found on a collective level. There are approximately 20,000 communes, between one and two hundred central living groups (large groups of independent households sharing certain facilities), and 7,000 dweller organizations in the Netherlands (Turpijn 1988:108). Turpijn points out that before the middle of the nineteenth century, the building and maintenance of houses were the responsibility of the individual, not government or professional organizations.

In 1992, an in-depth study of the squatters of vacant H.L.M. (Habitations de Loyer Modereis—similar to public housing in the United States) apartments in and around Paris was undertaken by Guy Boudimbou of the Centre de Recherche sur l'Habitat in Nanterre, France. The squatters in his study were primarily immigrants and their children from Northern and Western Africa.

Initially, foreign workers were encouraged to come to France in order to fill jobs. These workers were often single men who lived in any available furnished room, hotel, hostel, or shantytowns that had grown up. However, since the 1970s immigrants have included whole families, whose needs are for larger and more permanent housing. At the same time, the squatter towns outside of Paris were destroyed, in part a result of the well-publicized death of five Senegalese workers who lived there.

The African immigrant faces stigmatization and discrimination, which results in restrictions on his housing.

Public and private housing management, under the pretext of preventing the growth of ghettos, controls the location and number of units rented to Africans. During the 1970s, as the middle class left public housing and were able to buy their own housing, at least some of these immigrants entered public housing.

Because of the continuing difficulties involved in obtaining housing, especially for the newest African immigrants to France, squatting is currently taking place in various deteriorated public-housing units. The phenomenon appears to occur among both illegal and naturalized citizens, whose countries of origin include Zaire, Congo, Algeria, the Antilles, and Senegal. Some of the squatters are unemployed young people, but many are families. Squatter wage-earning families occasionally try to become regular tenants by proving their ability to pay rent. There have been cases where the management refuses to recognize them as legitimate tenants, *after* taking their money.

The system of squatting has its own perverse effects. One is the practice of unscrupulous "managers" who draw up a file of vacant apartments and offer individual apartments to two or three different families, each of whom thinks that the apartment is their own. After helping the first family get installed, the manager leaves them to fight for the apartment when the other families arrive. He, in return, gets away with the 2000 to 3000 francs that he collected from each family.

> One interviewee told us about the misadventure of a neighboring Algerian family, who upon returning from vacation, found its apartment occupied by strangers. Their belongings, representing some value, had been sold. This type of mistake can be frequent because an apartment not lit up or with windows without curtains for two weeks is supposedly empty and ready to be an "offer." (Boudimbou 1992:8)

The restrictive housing practices of the H.L.M., as seen in the study by Guy Boudimbou, have produced the unintended consequence of encouraging a network of squatters who move from one vacant building to another, without permanent residence. Squatting is seen as a consequence of the long-term neglect of the housing needs of immigrant families.

Health Issues

> [Bombay, India] The apparent vigor of the colorful and cheerful street crowds in the bazaars of Kurla and along the Visanji Road in Sakinaka belies the fact that the general health of the population is deplorably low. . . . Deep in these shanty towns, the line is not so clear between severe diarrhea, dysentery, and cholera, and the last is always lurking in the blocked community latrines, leaking sewer pipes (in the few places where they exist), and the many hectares of fetid shrubbery or kilometers of ditches where human and animal feces steadily accumulate throughout the long dry season, only to be spread throughout the whole area in the monsoon. (Eyre 1990:139–140)

In both the industrialized world and the developing world, the marginally housed are at risk for infectious diseases, respiratory diseases, and malnutrition (Novick 1987).

In an overview of the relationship between shelter and health, Robert E. Novick of the World Health Organization (1987) discusses the health consequences of a lack of adequate water supply for drinking and personal cleanliness, inadequate removal or disposal of excreta, insect and rodent infestations, unsupervised food markets, and excessive air and noise pollution. Novick estimates that these conditions affect approximately 1 billion people living in slums and squatter settlements throughout the world, leading to disease, as well as malnutrition and undernourishment, which further weakens the body's resistance to infection.

A lack of clean water and sanitary facilities combines to transmit disease. For example, many communicable diseases are transmitted when fecal matter, containing pathogenic organisms, contaminates food, water, or fingers and is ingested. Children are especially vulnerable to diarrhea, a condition that leads to severe dehydration and possibly death. It is estimated that one-third of all the deaths of children under 5 occur because of diarrheal disease (Novick 1987). The annual mortality rate of children in developing countries is estimated at about 15 million, with 50 percent of the deaths occurring in children under 5 years old.

Another consequence of diarrhea is that nutrients are poorly absorbed, increasing malnutrition and causing wasting (less than expected weight for age). An effect of chronic malnutrition is stunting (being short for one's age) (McElroy and Townsend 1989:216). Severe calorie and protein deficiency can cause a condition called marasmus, which leads to growth retardation, severe emaciation, and muscle atrophy (McElroy and Townsend 1989:208).

In Zimbabwe, a country with an estimated 85 percent of rural communities having neither safe water nor proper sanitation disposal, a successful campaign has been launched to eradicate these problems (Taylor 1987). Employing the Blair latrine, which has a vent pipe fitted with a fly-screen of fiberglass or stainless steel and can be used as an effective and odorless family toilet, the program combines government aid (the government supplies the cement and the fly-screen) and family labor. The Blair latrines have been widely accepted, helping to prevent the transmission of schistosomiasis, a disease in which parasitic worms infect blood vessels and tissues. Also, communities are digging pipelines and protecting boreholes for safe water.

Poor indoor air quality is another health hazard. Smoke and soot from fire used for cooking or heating and from burning substances such as charcoal or animal dung produce harmful toxins that cause acute respiratory infections (Novick 1987). Research in the shantytowns of Bombay illustrates the issue of both indoor and outdoor air pollution:

For a visitor the initial impact of the choking odor of garbage, excreta, and sulfur compounds is a never-to-be-forgotten experience. For the resident, this is not just a hazard, but a fact of life. The effluents from several thousand factories, power stations, and chemical plants cover these particular shanty towns with an almost permanent blanket of toxic sulfur and nitrogen oxides, fly ash, and a host of particulates. . . . (Eyre 1990:140)

A wide range of health and safety issues is linked to conditions in the welfare hotel. The inadequacy of toilet facilities, problems of sharing and overuse, and inadequate cleaning are directly linked to bouts of sickness, weight loss, and the faster development of latent health conditions. The lack of kitchen, cooking, and food-storage facilities forces families to rely on what is an expensive as well as an unhealthy way of living. Pressure on budgets also arises from lack of laundry and especially drying facilities for clothes (Murie and Forrest 1988: 140–141).

Programs and Policies for Homeless Families

Although it is not possible to mention every type of program for the homeless family, certain categories may briefly be described. Essentially, programs either increase the number of units of affordable housing, improve the person's ability to rent or own such housing, prevent the loss of housing, or advocate for the right of all people to housing.

Innovative Housing Construction

In northwest Nova Scotia, an attempt was made to increase the number of affordable rentals through the Hearth Home Project (Daly 1990b). The farmers of the area lived in shacks made from salvaged materials, including truck and bus bodies. In order to create more housing for them, the Housing Assistance Non-Profit Development Society offered housing congruent with their resources and life-styles. The housing was planned with these characteristics of the area and people in mind: ". . . wood is available locally and is the traditional source of heat; families spend most of the time in the kitchen, cooking, eating, and socializing; and most do not want or need a 'standard' National Housing Agency-approved home" (Daly 1990b:141).

By 1990, fifty-three homes, renting at $350 per month, were built. Made of wood, containing two bedrooms, a living room, and bath, and featuring a large eat-in kitchen, the total cost of each house was $44,000, which could be paid through a mortgage with the Nova Scotia Department of Housing.

The Undugu Society in Kenya has helped build 1,068 houses in three squatter communities in Nairobi—Kitui, Kanuku, and Kinyago—all settlements with "igloo" huts of cardboard and plastic, subject to frequent fires and the constant threat of eviction (Settlements Information Network Africa 1986a). The Undugu Society stressed community participation in the planning and building of the new houses, utilizing the skills and resources of each community's young people, women, and elderly for some of the leadership. The new houses were made of locally available mud, branches, and homemade nails, with the Undugu Society contributing iron roofs and tools. Community buildings such as a nursery school and community hall were also constructed. The cost of a typical house was U.S. $280, with the Society contributing approximately two-thirds and the local residents one-third of the amount. The biggest problems still faced by these communities are land security and sanitation.

Transitional Housing

One approach to helping homeless families become and stay housed is "transitional housing," as it is known in the United States. Transitional housing has been defined as

> a multi-family residency program that includes a variety of support services for low-income women who are heads of households and for their children. It is sometimes called *second stage* housing to distinguish its place after crisis or homeless shelter, providing the bridge for women to self-sufficiency and permanent housing. The residency period has a variable but finite duration, generally from six months to two years. (Women's Institute for Housing and Economic Development, Inc. 1986:4)

In the United States transitional housing was first discussed during the mid-1980s, when the same women and children were continually readmitted to homeless shelters—often termed the "revolving door effect." Transitional housing programs take in women from homeless shelters and doubled-up situations or women who are at high risk for homelessness, such as those released from prison. The term appears to be a generic one, encompassing programs ranging from those that offer counseling and tenant–landlord liaison work to those (more common) that provide separate apartments for women and children, with counseling and some shared spaces.

An example of transitional housing is the Thames River Family Program in Norwich, Connecticut, which administers a modern multistory building containing twenty-four apartments for women and their children (Suroviak 1993). The program is located several miles outside of town, but is on the bus lines to the small city of Norwich. For families on AFDC, the cost rarely exceeds $100 a month. The families must agree to the rules of the program, which include living in a drug, alcohol, and violence free community; keeping the apartment clean; and attending off-site education or job training programs. Transitional housing is appropriate for women who not only want shelter but are motivated to participate in counseling and training for economic self-sufficiency.

Mediation: A Program That Helps People Keep Their Housing

Another approach to helping families keep their housing is to avoid evictions, which constitute one of the major causes of homelessness in the United States. One such program is the Tenancy Settlement/ Mediation Program, which appears to be having success in Passaic County, New Jersey, an area with a declining amount of residential housing, a deteriorating economic base, and high rates of poverty and public assistance. The program is staffed by social workers who are trained in mediation (Curcio 1992). The settlement/mediation program serves sixteen municipalities with a combined population of 500,000 people.

Nonpayment of rent, one of the most common reasons for eviction, is often handled by the program:

> In nonpayment-of-rent complaints, the mediators attempt to work out payment schedules so that tenants may keep their apartments and landlords may receive over a period of time all monies due them. Many times, repairs and refurbishment timetables are also built into the schedules so as to simultaneously address issues of habitability.

> Paramount in the mediation process is the goal of restoring the land-
> lord–tenant relationship. (Curcio 1992:37)

The impact of the program is substantial. In 1990, approximately 1,300
tenancy disputes, involving 3,600 adults and children, were successfully settled, representing an 89.5 percent success rate. Of the people
involved in the cases, 55 percent were on fixed incomes or public assistance, and 45 percent were employed full- or part-time. It appears that,
had they not been successfully mediated, at least some of these eviction cases would have ended up in homelessness or doubling-up for the
tenants involved.

Squatter Upgrading and Sites and Services Projects

Throughout the Third World, programs exist that enable squatter settlements to upgrade their housing, bring in essential services (potable
water, sanitation, and electricity), and secure the right to remain in
housing. Nongovernmental agencies (NGOs) as well as governmental
agencies have been involved in this effort.

The World Bank is one of the leaders in the lending of money for
sites and services projects and squatter upgrading projects. A model
used by the World Bank is known as "progressive development," which
implies that improvements in housing should be made at a pace congruent with the incomes and preferences of the households involved.
There is flexibility in the materials of construction and how the self-
help component is embodied in the project. In some parts of the world,
households help to build each other's houses; in other regions, the
household hires people to work for it; in still others, the household
builds the house on its own (Keare and Parris 1982).

A successful example of squatter upgrading is the Kampung
Improvement Programme in Jakarta, Indonesia (Oliver 1987). In
Jakarta, the word *kampung* refers to urban settlements constructed on
swampy land, built with floors of earth, and subject to serious flooding.
A 1969 survey found that out of 4.5 million people in Jakarta 65 percent
had no toilets and 80 percent had no electricity. The Kampung
Improvement Programme provided 87 *kampungs* (over one million peo-
ple) with clean water, canals to mitigate flooding, improved roads and
concrete paths, communal sanitation, and a system of garbage disposal.
A World Bank Loan in 1974 also provided for schools and health clinics.

A major finding of this project was that bringing in services to the community inspired individual householders to improve their dwellings on their own.

Advocacy

Advocacy groups for the homeless gather documentation, publicize the plight of the homeless, and press for concrete programs and funds to increase the availability of housing. These advocacy groups are most often local or regional, though some are national and a few are international. For example, a group called Unnayan acts as an information center for the National Campaign for Housing Rights, an independent, non-profit, social-action organization based in Calcutta. *Unnayan* is the Bengali word for development. Since 1977 the group has concentrated on campaigning for the right to housing, helping groups fight evictions, and providing research and documentation concerning housing. An example of the work of Unnayan is their 1991 analysis of the election manifestos of six political parties in India on the issue of housing (National Campaign for Housing Rights 1991).

An example of an international advocacy group is the Habitat International Coalition (HIC), based in Mexico City, which addresses itself in part to the role of women in homelessness:

> Among the local actors [participants] HIC advances the leading role of women in struggles for housing and services and against evictions because they are the ones most affected. The maintenance of shelter, basic services such as water, fuel, food preparation, health care, physical and household hygiene, and washing remain perceived as women's responsibilities. (Habitat International Coalition 1992:6)

Homeless families present us with the most diverse interpretation of homelessness in the world. From families in shelters and hotels to squatters and pavement dwellers, homeless families lack the tools with which to protect themselves from the outside world or to nurture and educate their children. Eventually, homeless families lose their ability to function as a family, and many fall apart. Adequate and secure housing is essential in keeping families together; it is the anchor that underlies the concept of "family" itself.

6

Counting the Homeless

If not all, some look at us suspiciously as we attempt to start a conversation with them, regarding their work, ways of life and reasons for houselessness. Most fear to part with their personal information while some are in a hurry to go to sleep as their so-called beds are already laid on the pavements. It is around midnight. You cannot catch them earlier. Only a few respond and that too for a few minutes.

We first stationed ourselves in a cluster of people called "garbage pickers" in the vicinity of the Red Fort of Shah Jahan. These houseless people pick up waste paper from the garbage and sell it to the wholesale junk-seller (*kabaris*) to earn their livelihood.

Though it was mid-night and most people were asleep, a young boy was still busy picking from a nearby garbage bin in the dim street light.

"What's there in the garbage which allures you at this odd hour of night?"

Many things! Waste paper, cardboard, plastic chappals, old shoes, bones and what not. This sweep provides us an easy living. Not only me, many others in age group 15 to 40 have taken to picking as our mainstay. All these items fetch a good price." (Gandotra 1977:31)

One of the most difficult tasks in the study of homelessness is counting homeless individuals accurately. The answer to the common question of "how many are homeless?" depends on: (1) the definition(s) of homelessness used and (2) the rigors (and expense) of an enumeration. Some

Homeless child, Nicaragua.

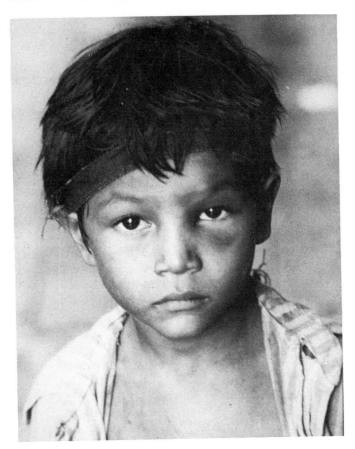

UNICEF/Peter Taçon.

nations such as the United States and India approach the homeless count within the framework of the national decennial census. The problem with a census is that it is traditionally accomplished on the basis of *domicile* (or dwelling), so that to count the *undomiciled* requires a different methodology. Also, the homeless themselves are a changing group of people. Taking a "slice in time" photo of them on a single night (as is the case in a census) is quite different and produces a much smaller number than asking how many were homeless at any time during an entire year. Nonetheless, using the census is better than doing nothing at all, which is the case in many countries.

The idea of a national census is very old, and there is evidence that population censuses took place as early as 30 centuries B.C.E in ancient Babylonia, China, and Egypt (see Srivastava 1983, for a brief overview of the census in international perspective). The counting of an entire population can be a highly controversial undertaking, since the results are used to allocate political representation and services to areas or groups within the country. There may be problems of undercounting as well as overcounting (counting the same person twice or more). In 1991, in an attempt to take an accurate census of its population, Nigeria closed its borders, shut down businesses and schools, and stopped international travel into and out of the country so that people would stay home and be counted (Noble 1991). These measures were taken due to the lack of success of three previous post–independence censuses. The counting of specific populations within a national census can be flawed, as appears to be the case in the undercounting of the black and Hispanic populations within the United States (de la Puente 1990).

The United States Census

In the 1990 decennial census of the United States, components of the homeless population were systematically counted. In addition, there were several independent evaluation studies sponsored by the Bureau of the Census that attempted to evaluate the accuracy and comprehensiveness of the count. The Bureau also sponsored ethnographic studies of the homeless in order to refine the methodology of the census (see Glasser 1991).

The literally homeless (those living outdoors and in shelters) were counted in a special enumeration on March 20, 1990, eleven days before the regular count on April 1. This was known as the S-Night (shelter and street) count. The instructions for S-Night were:

> First, we will conduct one special operation ("shelter and street night") on March 20, 1990 to count persons in *pre-identified* emergency shelters (public and private) and open locations in the streets or other places not intended for habitation. This special operation includes all hotels/motels

costing $12 or less per night, hotels/motels used entirely to shelter the homeless (regardless of cost), and pre-identified rooms in hotels/motels used for homeless persons and families. Enumeration will occur when the population is generally settled for the night. For shelters, enumeration will usually occur from 6 p.m. to midnight; street enumeration, from 2 a.m. to 4 a.m. (U.S. Department of Commerce, Bureau of the Census 1990b)

Further instructions to the enumerators included not waking up sleeping people, but only noting their race, gender, and approximate age; not entering abandoned buildings, but waiting outside these buildings from 4 A.M. to 8 A.M. to meet the people who had been sleeping inside; and not counting people on the street who were in uniform (such as police) or who were obviously engaged in money-making activities (by which was meant drug dealing and prostitution), but to include people involved in begging and panhandling who were at the pre-identified place. It was stressed to the census takers not to try to make judgments about who was homeless and who was not, but to count *everyone* in the places that had been identified by the local municipality or county as sites where the homeless could be found at night. The Bureau of the Census knew that, with this methodology, they would not be able to include the homeless who were well hidden, moving about, or in other than the pre-identified locations. There was a separate count for women in shelters for domestic violence, as well as for those people who had "no usual home elsewhere" (this is the official phrase), residing in halfway houses, maternity homes, agricultural workers' dormitories, commercial campgrounds, and other nonhousehold living situations.

The "doubled-up population," thought to be substantial by many advocacy groups, was to be counted within the regular April 1 census. As defined by the Census Bureau, the doubled-up were "persons living in somebody else's home because they cannot afford, or temporarily do not have, their own accommodations. There is a general sense that both the original household and the secondary household are relatively poor and that living conditions are crowded" (Miskura 1989:1).

When filling out the census form, hosts of doubled-up apartments or houses were directed to include in their form all those staying with them who had nowhere else to go. There was an additional section where the respondent was asked to write in the names of persons whom they were unsure about including in their census form. These doubled-up families are sometimes referred to as "subfamilies," who may or may not be related to the original household. The Census Bureau, in its analysis of the 1990 Census, was able to make a gross inference of the existence of doubled-up persons and families, although they avoided making an actual count of this category (Miskura 1989; Taeuber and Siegel 1990).

The final numbers of homeless people in 1990, as released by the Bureau of the Census, were 178,638 persons in emergency shelters and 49,734 persons visible at pre-identified street locations (U.S. Department of Commerce, Bureau of the Census 1990a). The total of 228,372 was closer to the HUD (Department of Housing and Urban Development) estimate of between 250,000 and 350,000 homeless people in 1984 but considerably below the estimate of two to three million presented by advocacy groups throughout the 1980s (Wright and Devine 1992). The total U.S. population reported for 1990 was 248,709,873 (U.S. Department of Commerce, Bureau of the Census 1992).

The Census Bureau's evaluation of the *shelter count* of the S-Night effort, based on its own work and that of an independent study, was that it was for the most part accurate. The lists of shelters were reasonably complete, and shelter staff and residents were cooperative. There is some evidence that some shelters opened on a temporary basis just for the count.

On the other hand, there were various problems with the quality of the data for the *street count*, a conclusion that was based on both the Bureau's own evaluation and those of the five independent S-Night observation projects that had been contracted in five cities in the United States by the Bureau of the Census's Center for Survey Methods Research (see *Evaluation Review* 16 [4], August 1992, for a complete discussion of these five projects). Among the problems that may have led to an underestimate of the number of homeless on the street were the unusually cold and wet weather on March 20, which may have forced the homeless into shelters or well-hidden locations; the presence of the media, which in some places was obtrusive and violated the confidentiality that the Bureau tried to insure; the failure of some of the enumerators to find the locations; the special efforts that were made by some communities to have the homeless enter shelters for the purpose of being counted; and the propensity of some of the enumerators not to leave their cars to interview the homeless (Taeuber and Siegel 1990;

Wright and Devine 1992). Contrary to instructions, some enumerators did ask people if they were homeless, and others appeared to make those decisions themselves (based, presumably, on the physical appearance of the person).

One of the most interesting approaches to the evaluation of the street count was the use of "decoys"—unobtrusive observers who positioned themselves in a sample of the pre-identified sites in the five observation projects (New York, Los Angeles, Chicago, Phoenix, and New Orleans). Since the enumerators had been instructed to count *everyone* in the pre-identified sites, all the decoys should have been interviewed, or at least counted. The dummy enumeration forms of the decoys would then be subtracted from the final street counts.

The number of observers who reported being interviewed or definitely counted (as opposed to possibly counted) on S-Night at the sampled sites was low overall—77 percent in New Orleans, 54 percent in New York, 52 percent in Phoenix, 35 percent in Los Angeles, and 25 percent in Chicago (Martin 1992). However, a higher percentage of the observers reported seeing the census enumerators—95 percent in New Orleans, 86 percent in New York, 64 percent in Phoenix, 52 percent in Los Angeles, and 50 percent in Chicago. There are reasons for the relatively low rates of observers being counted in the 1990 census. Some of the enumerators had trouble finding the sites, and as mentioned previously, others were too afraid to leave their cars. In large, complex areas such as subway stations, the enumerators might not have been noticed by the observers. In order to insure that they could find the sites and to better organize the count, the enumerators should have visited their pre-identified areas of responsibility beforehand and in the daytime.

The Indian Census

India has also attempted to enumerate its houseless (the term for the homeless in India, as such people are viewed as living without a roof over their heads) population, including a count of the houseless in its national decennial census since at least 1961 (Gandotra 1977). Before then, 200 social workers had counted 6,000 houseless persons in Delhi in December 1954, in a census of pavement dwellers.

In the 1991 census, the instructions for the census workers included the following:

The enumeration of the houseless population will have to be carried out in the block assigned to you. The houseless population can be found in any place and they should not be omitted . . . you will be required to enumerate the houseless population in your enumeration block(s) on the night of February 28, 1991. In order to do this, it would be necessary for you to complete the enumeration of all the persons in all the households living in census houses in your jurisdiction between February 9 and February 28, 1991. During this period, you will have taken note of the possible places where the houseless population is likely to live, such as on the pavements, in hume pipes [old, unused cement sewer pipes], under staircases, in the open, temple mandaps, platforms and the like. On the night of February 28/March 1, 1991, but before sunrise of March 1, 1991, you will have to quickly cover all such houseless households and enumerate them. If there is likely to be a very large number of houseless persons in your jurisdiction whom you may not be able to enumerate single-handed in one night, you should report to your Supervisor in advance, so that one or more extra enumerators can be deputed to assist you in the one-night enumeration of such houseless persons. You should keep particular watch on the large settlements of the nomadic population who are likely to camp on the outskirts of the village. These people will have to be covered on the night of February 28, 1991. You should of course make sure that these persons have not been enumerated elsewhere. (Roa 1992)

In contrast to the homeless count in the United States, the enumerators of India have almost three weeks to get to know the areas in which the homeless live. Although the count is also done in one night (to avoid a duplicate count of the same person), the census takers are not working as "blindly" as the U.S. enumerators.

India's 1981 homeless census, the latest count available at this time, found that there were a total of 629,929 homeless households, which included 2,342,954 homeless persons. Seventy-four percent of the homeless population was rural and 26 percent urban. However, the rural/urban distribution reversed itself in states with major cities such as West Bengal and Delhi. The population of India for 1981 was reported at 683,810,057 (United Nations 1983).

The 1971 census in the state of Delhi indicated that there were 19,163 houseless persons (Gandotra 1977). This was a 191 percent increase in houselessness since the 1961 census of the same area, in contrast with an increase of 53 percent for the total population. A finding of this census was that 96 percent of the houseless females were illiterate (defined here as not being able to write in any language). In 1981 26,870 houseless individuals were counted in the state of Delhi (Roa 1992).

A published report of the 1971 census of Delhi includes case studies drawn from conversations with pavement dwellers (Gandotra 1977). An excerpt from one of the case studies reveals the information that may be obtained from even a brief encounter:

> Next we accosted a middle-aged man, Sube Singh. He was an agriculturist nearing 55 who had come to Delhi from a village in Uttar Pradesh to earn money for getting his daughter married and for repaying old debts. He was lying half asleep on a pavement and appeared much older than his age. In spite of our best efforts, we could not make him understand the purpose of our enquiry. At last, exasperated with continuous goading, he exploded, though of course timidly. "Babuji, who are you, asking all these very personal questions? Are you searching for a pick-pocket at dead of night?"
>
> "We are trying to study the problems of pavement dwellers like you. We are not policemen in disguise, nor searching for any pickpocket."
>
> After a pause, we enquired, "Do you sleep on the pavement round the year?"
>
> "Well, during the rainy season, I sleep here, under the shelter of this veranda, while in summer in any of the nearby parks. During the winters, I prefer to sleep in a somewhat enclosed place like the threshold of a house or on the stairs of an available building."
>
> "But in winter, you can sleep in any of the nearby night shelters run by the Municipal Corporation, without paying any charges."
>
> "You see, I am an aged villager, not acquainted with the ways of city life. I could not dare to ask the night shelter authorities for providing me a sleeping place." (Gandotra 1977: 32)

Enumeration Efforts of Other Nations

In addition to counting the homeless as a part of the national census, there have been attempts systematically to collect data about the homeless on a national scale. Finland, for example, has been gathering national data regarding homelessness since 1986 (Vesanen 1991).

In Finland, homeless people are defined as:

1) persons completely roofless, or living in temporary shelters or the like
2) persons living in common wards or casual lodgings due to   lack of own housing
3) persons temporarily accommodated by friends or relatives
4) family members living separately, due to lack of housing (Vesanen 1991:1)

The Finnish definition expands the concept of homelessness to include not only the visible homeless and those who live in shelters (as in the United States and India), but also the doubled-up homeless *and* the separated family. According to this definition, there were approximately 18,000 to 20,000 homeless single people and from 1,000 to 2,000 homeless families in Finland in 1990. Vesanen (1991) estimates that there are approximately three homeless persons per one thousand persons in Finland. The population of Finland for 1990 was reported as 4,910,619 (United Nations 1992).

Most of the homeless can be found in towns and in the capital city of Helsinki; many appear to have moved from the northern part of the country to the south in search of employment. The largest group of homeless persons in 1990 (ca. 8,000) consisted of people living with their friends and relatives and moving from one place to another.

In London, the Salvation Army sponsored two studies of the numbers of homeless, both of which were conducted by researchers from the University of Surrey (Canter 1988; Moore 1991). The first was a pilot count of the homeless of central London (an area of 1.75 miles) on November 22, 1988, that enumerated people in the following circumstances:

People living "rough" on the streets or "skippering" [living in houses without such amenities as water or electricity].
People in hostels and night shelters.
People in bed and breakfast hotels.
People in squats.
People with no fixed abode in hospital and police cells.
People doubled-up or living with friends—the "hidden homeless." (Canter 1988:1)

The area of the street count was divided into sections (called patches), each of which were canvassed by a team of three counters on the night of November 22, 1988. Employing a total of 100 volunteer counters, the strategy went as follows:

> Seventy counters set off at midnight to count their patches and all had returned safely by 3 a.m. Before embarking, counters were briefed on safety precautions and counting procedures. To obtain as much information as possible, counters were asked to mark a map they were given. They were further requested to describe in as much detail as possible the gender, age, ethnicity, and general state of health and any details of the surroundings in which they [the homeless persons] were found. Counters were given instructions not to put themselves at risk by, for example, entering derelict buildings. Thus, while it is known that people do sleep in such buildings, they are not included in this count. (Canter 1988:2)

The hostel and night shelter residents of the pilot area were counted by having the staff fill out a form on the number of residents present that night and also the number of empty beds. Bed and breakfast hotels were enumerated on November 23 by having questionnaires filled out by the hotel management and included the area just outside the street count boundaries (there were no hotels in the street count area). Squatters were located through a network of squatter advocacy groups. They were enumerated by filling out a questionnaire themselves. It appears that care was taken to protect the confidentiality (and presumably location) of the squatters, since they were living in abandoned houses illegally. Finally, hospital and police stations were canvassed to find people who had stayed overnight and had "no fixed abode" as an address.

The pilot count found 271 people to be living on the street and 1,349 people to be staying in the fourteen hostels of the area, which had forty-eight empty beds (a student hostel that took in homeless people had another 307 residents). Fifty hotels were visited by the counters, who found that twenty-six of them took homeless people—there were a total of 419 people residing in these hotels. Thirty-four individuals responded to the squatter questionnaire, and seven people had registered no fixed abode as their address in the police stations and hospitals of the area.

The researchers approached these numbers with caution, since they did not get 100 percent cooperation from all of the services for the homeless, and they felt that many of the homeless were hidden from view. According to the researchers' estimates, there were approximately five people in hostels and bed and breakfast hotels for every one person on the streets of central London on November 22, 1988.

A second study by the same research team on April 25, 1989, expanded the area of study to seventeen boroughs in London. The estimated numbers of homeless from the 1989 study were 2,000 on the street; 18,000 in hostels; 25,000 in squats; and 75,000 total (Moore 1991:3). The London population for 1989 was reported at 6,735,353 (United Nations 1991).

In Ibadan, Nigeria, a systematic count of homeless people took place between June and July, 1987, during the peak of the rainy season (Labeodan 1989). The research was based on interviews, structured questionnaires, and field observations. A night survey was also conducted between 10 P.M. and 12 midnight in an area known as the "homeless haven in Ibadan." In all, a total of 1,650 people were found to be without homes (not including those in marginal housing). The projected number of homeless in Ibadan, based on this sample, was 15,735 (Labeodan 1989:79). The population of the city during the same year was reported as 847,000 (United Nations 1989).

A brief description of the homeless of Ibadan follows:

> The homeless found in these areas sleep on road kerbs, pavements, inside old train coaches/vehicles (*danfo*—buses) and in front of closed market stalls. It was found that night guards harbour some of these homeless persons under the pretext that they too are guards. They [the homeless] play cards till about 2 a.m. and then sleep on benches or tables. In the morning they go begging for alms or work as load carriers. (Labeodan 1989:79)

Two hundred of the homeless people in this study were interviewed. It was found that the majority (86 percent) were below 40 years of age, and of these, 35 percent were under 20 years; the largest percentage (84 percent) had no more than a sixth-grade education; and 4 percent were identified as "call girls." The study suggested that the government establish a homeless person unit within the Ministry of Information, Social Development, Welfare and Sports, so that the coordination of support and services for the homeless be better organized;

that a rent subsidy be given to the poorest of the homeless; and that the government invest more money in housing for the homeless (Labeodan 1989:83–84).

June 4 Count Yourself In! - Soyez du nombre! 4 juin
CENSUS DAY - RECENSEMENT

Using this bilingual slogan to rally its citizenry, Canada took a census of its population on June 4, 1991, describing the census as "the latest portrait of Canada" (Statistics Canada n.d.). Although Statistics Canada, the governmental bureau in charge of the census, did not plan to enumerate the homeless separately, census data were collected in shelters and soup kitchens in order to improve the census counts of the entire Canadian population (Boyko 1992; Statistics Canada n.d.). All persons staying overnight in shelters between June 3 and June 4, 1991, were asked to fill out an individual census questionnaire and return it to the shelter manager. On June 4, persons using soup kitchens in sixteen cities filled out a special "soup-kitchen enumeration" questionnaire. In both cases, people were asked about their "usual residence" and were asked if they had already filled out a census questionnaire somewhere else. For those people who had a residence elsewhere or who indicated that they had already been counted, a tracing operation was conducted to see if they had indeed been counted, in order to eliminate double counting. For those people in the soup kitchens who refused to fill out the census form or talk to the interviewer, the interviewer completed a questionnaire to indicate only whether the person was male or female and to estimate his or her age.

The methodology of Statistics Canada did not include homeless persons who did not visit a shelter or soup kitchen on the dates of the census. Also, there were people in soup kitchens who were not homeless (although these people would have had a chance to indicate that they were included in the census in their household). Statistics Canada planned to release some aggregate data regarding the shelter and soup kitchen count in late 1992.

The problems of obtaining an accurate count of "the homeless" are enormous. Many enumeration efforts begin with a count of people in shelters, hostels, and hotels specifically designated for the homeless, but even this method is fraught with problems. Many places are too small or too transient to be listed as homeless shelters, and residences such as hotels serve as a homeless shelter for some and as a permanent abode for others. Efforts that confine themselves to people admitted to shelters and other services for the homeless only count those who have presented themselves for admission *and* been accepted. Given the many overt and covert screens with which shelters operate, this might indeed be a select group that is counted.

A count taken out-of-doors is fraught with even more problems. Many homeless people, as a safety precaution, hide themselves from view. Others move around throughout the night, when street counts are typically performed. People recruited to enumerate the homeless are often unfamiliar with the streets, and so are easily lost or frightened. Even when one can get a reasonably accurate street count of a small area, it is not necessarily correct to extrapolate the number to a wider area, since sections of any city are more or less hospitable to homeless people.

Finally, families who are doubled-up with other families, families divided due to a lack of housing, and families who are squatting in abandoned buildings may be the most difficult to enumerate. They may also represent the largest numbers of people who are homeless.

In spite of all of the challenges of enumeration, there is much to be learned from an even less-than-ideal homeless count, as long as a systematic methodology is employed. The process itself is a way to draw attention to people who are out of sight and mind from the rest of society.

7
Conclusion

Homelessness and hunger are the two most palpable indications of poverty, as well as the clearest indications of society's inability to care even minimally for its most vulnerable members. Homelessness, as we have seen, has a wide range of meanings in world perspective, from the pavement dwellers on the streets of Bombay, to the shelter dwellers of New York City, to the squatters in vacant apartments in London, to the "igloo" residents of Nairobi. Homelessness also has many different definitions in world perspective. For example, in Finland, the official definition of homelessness includes not only people in shelters, living outside, and doubled-up with other families, but people who are currently living apart from one another because of a lack of housing. Perhaps Finland can "afford" more inclusive categories of homelessness because it has relatively few truly homeless people, in contrast to a country with thousands of literally roofless people, such as India.

In addition to definitional differences, there are varying degrees of our knowledge about the homeless. For example, in most of the world, homeless women either do not exist or (more probably) are not acknowledged or written about. When there is a lack of research, there is also a wider lack of interest, which results in lack of documentation with which to justify the funding of housing and programs. On the other hand, a long tradition of research exists about the homeless man, who is discussed as either being sick and lonely, fiercely independent, piously beggarly, or deranged and dangerous. While our scant knowledge of single homeless women comes from the industrialized world, the research on homeless men is more universal, as descriptions of the "vagrant psychotic" in Africa, the cage apartment dwellers of Hong Kong, and the homeless former *yoseba* residents of Japan make clear.

In the case of both homeless single men and homeless single women, the most successful programs require the availability of affordable housing as well as techniques for weaning people off the streets that begin with low-key approaches that respect the individual's own survival strategies. Chez Doris in Montreal and the Manhattan Bowery Corporation start by offering food, a shower, a place to rest, and the possibility of communicating with other homeless people. Those who work in "rescue" operations offered by organizations such as the Salvation Army know that it is impossible to determine in advance which homeless man or woman may be most interested in getting off the streets. Therefore, even those services that focus on *survival* by offering food and temporary shelter must have knowledgeable staff who can recognize a cry for help. Once a person does become interested in more permanent housing, projects such as the Veteran's Manor in Vancouver are successful in offering permanent housing in a neighborhood in which the formerly homeless are comfortable.

The richest and most abundant homeless literature focuses on homeless children, who, whether on the street, in large and impersonal orphanages, or in shelters or welfare hotels, are subject to unhealthful and sometimes violent conditions. The street child is usually not attending school, so that he or she lacks preparation for a productive adulthood. The less connection children have with their parents, the greater their vulnerability. Those advocacy efforts that stress the needs of street children, rather than the criminal activities to which some of them resort for survival, are most successful. As is the case in working with homeless men and women, the most exemplary projects begin by offering the children food, temporary shelter, recreation, and some schooling, within their own milieu on the streets.

The literature on homeless families stresses the lack of adequate housing for poor families, as opposed to concentrating on the characteristics of the people themselves. A minimum standard of shelter with clean water and waste disposal is necessary for the healthy rearing of children and the productivity of the family. Projects that increase the availability of housing in the most culturally congruent manner, with the most reliance on the residents themselves, are the most successful.

Street school, Brazil.

UNICEF/William Hetzer.

While most countries do not attempt to count the homeless within their national census, India has what appears to be an effective methodology for a homeless count. There is a striking contrast between the United States homeless enumerator who tries to locate the homeless person in the dead of night, in a neighborhood with which he is unfamiliar, and the Indian enumerator who has three weeks in which to study the living arrangements of the homeless.

Much of the best research presented in this book has been in-depth, longitudinal research that follows an individual or family over time. The difficulty of finding an apartment in New York City comes to life when we watch the Carter family make their way through the shelter and welfare hotel system. The plight of the world's street children is revealed through the labor of project workers in Latin America who contact children in their own environments, providing refuge, food, and medical care and coming to know the children and their families over time. We can see the shortcomings of the quick shelter survey, which studies only those homeless who have chosen or been accepted by particular service providers. Some of the best research is an outgrowth of such service projects as the Health Care for the Homeless Program in the United States, which was able to document the health status of thousands of homeless men, women, children, and families.

It is obvious that the most effective way to address homelessness is to prevent it from happening in the first place. Families must be provided with the tools to support their children so that the children are not pushed out into the street. Governments must invest in more social housing (the term used in Canada and Australia for housing schemes that range from public housing to cooperative housing) so that poor families are not victimized by market forces. Housing, like other basic needs such as health care, needs more guarantees. If an individual loses a job, his entire well-being should not be in jeopardy. The programs for the homeless that reinforce the creativity and resourcefulness of the family, such as the squatter upgrading projects and the sites and services projects of the developing world, have served as a model for some of the more innovative cooperative building projects of the industrialized world.

It is clear that homelessness is not compatible with either the health or the well-being of the homeless individual or family. It is equally clear that it is not compatible with the rest of society. Global perspectives such as this serve to enlighten us with the critical importance of safe and secure housing for all.

Appendix

Recommended Readings

Austerberry, Helen, and Sophie Watson (1983). *Women on the margins: A study of single women's housing problems*. London: Housing Research Group, The City University.

Bassuk, Ellen, Lenore Rubin, and Alison Lauriat (1986). Characteristics of sheltered homeless families. *American Journal of Public Health 76*(9):1097–1101.

Baxter, E., and K. Hopper (1981). *Private lives/public spaces: Homeless adults on the streets of New York City*. New York: Community Service Society.

Cohen, Carol I., and Jay Sokolovsky (1989). *Old men of the Bowery: Strategies for survival among the homeless*. New York: Guilford Press.

Daly, Gerald (1990a). "Health implications of homelessness: Reports from three countries. *Journal of Sociology and Social Welfare 27*(1):111–125.

_____ (1990b). Programs dealing with homelessness in the United States, Canada and Britain. In Jamshid Momeni (Ed.), *Homelessness in the United States: Data and issues* (pp. 133–152). New York: Praeger.

Das, Bidyut K. (1986). *The rural poor in the city: A study on social transformation among the pavement dwellers in Calcutta*. Calcutta: Anthropological Survey of India, Government of India.

De Jesus, Carolina Maria (1963). *Child of the dark: The diary of Carolina Maria De Jesus*. Translated from the Portuguese. New York: New American Library.

Eyre, L. Alan (1990). The shanty towns of central Bombay. *Urban Geography 11*(2):130–152.

Fallis, George, and Alex Murray (Eds.) (1990). *Housing the homeless and poor*. Toronto: University of Toronto Press.

Fitchen, Janet M. (1991). *Endangered spaces, enduring places: Change, identity and survival in rural America*. Boulder: Westview.

Gandotra, S. R. (1977). *Census of India: Special study—Houseless in Delhi*. New Delhi: Director of Census Operations.

Glasser, Irene (1988). *More than bread: Ethnography of a soup kitchen*. Tuscaloosa: University of Alabama Press.

Gugler, Josef (Ed.) (1988). *The urbanization of the Third World*. Oxford: Oxford University Press.

Hardoy, Jorge E., and David Satterthwaite (1989). *Squatter citizen: Life in the urban Third World*. London: Earthscan Publications.

Kozol, J. (1988). *Rachel and her children: Homeless families in America*. New York: Crown.

McAuslan, Patrick (1985). *Urban land and shelter for the poor*. London and Washington, DC: Earthscan International Institute for Environment and Development.

Rossi, Peter H. (1989). *Down and out in America*. Chicago: University of Chicago Press.

Rousseau, Ann Marie (1981). *Shopping bag ladies*. New York: Pilgrim Press.

Rowe, Stacy, and Jennifer Wolch (1990). Social networks in time and space: Homeless women in skid row, Los Angeles. *Annals of the Association of American Geographers 80*(2):184–204.

Spradley, James (1970). *You owe yourself a drunk: An ethnography of urban nomads*. Boston: Little, Brown.

Stoner, Madeleine R. (1983). The plight of homeless women. *Social service review 57*(4):565–581.

United Nations Centre for Human Settlements (1990). *Shelter: From projects to national strategies. International Year of Shelter for the Homeless*. Nairobi.

Ward, J. (1989). *Organizing for the homeless*. Ottawa/Montreal Canadian Council on Social Development.

Wiseman, Jacqueline (1970). *Stations of the lost*. Chicago: University of Chicago Press.

Wright, James D. (Ed.) (1992). Counting the homeless. *Evaluation Review: A journal of applied social research 16*(4) (Entire issue).

Recommended Videos

Back Wards to Back Streets
Film Makers Library
124 E. 40 Street
New York, NY
1980

Excellent portrayal of deinstitutionalization in New York State and some of the subsequent problems of life on the streets for the formerly institutionalized, chronically mentally ill.

Inside Life Outside
West Glenn Films
New York, NY
1988

Interesting ethnographic-style presentation of a small group of squatters living on an empty lot in the Bronx.

My Sky, My Home (1990, director, Eros Djarot)
Asian Pacific Film Tour
East/West Center
Institute of Culture and Communication
1777 East/West Road
Honolulu, Hawaii 96848

A child from the *kampung* (squatter settlement) of Jakarta, Indonesia, meets a child from an upper-middle-class family.

Pixote (1981, director, Hector Babenco)
Embrafilms, RCA/Columbia Picture Home Video
3500 W. Olive Avenue
Burbank, CA 91505

Feature-length fictionalized account of abandoned children in a Brazilian institution and on the streets outside.

Salaam Bombay (1986, director, Mira Nair)
Image Entertainment
Virgin Home Entertainment
9333 Oso Avenue
Chatsworth, CA 91311

Feature-length fictionalized account of a street child in Bombay, India.

Streetwise (1988, directors Mary Ellen Mark, Martin Bell, and Cheryl McCall)
New World Video
1440 S. Sepulveda Boulevard
Los Angeles, CA 90025

Excellent ethnographic-style film about teenagers on the streets of Seattle, Washington.

References

Adams, Carolyn T. (1986). Homelessness in the postindustrial city: Views from London and Philadelphia. *Urban Affairs Quarterly 21* (4 June):527–49.

Adarkwa, Kwasi (1987). Where eight share one room. *World Health* (July): 20–21.

Advisory Service for Squatters (1987). *Squatters Handbook*. London.

_____ (1990). Squatting in London now: Press and media briefing. London.

Alexander, Maggie (1991). Promising program models: People power for street children: Lessons from the Philippines. *Esperanza 3*:5.

Allsop, Kenneth (1972). *Hard travellin': The hobo and his history*. Middlesex: Penguin.

Amnesty International, U.S.A. (1990). *Children: The youngest victims*. Compilation of Amnesty International documents and articles concerning human rights abuses of children. New York.

Anderson, Nels (1923). *The hobo*. Chicago: University of Chicago Press.

Appleby, Lawrence, Nancy Slagg, and Prakash N. Desai (1982). The urban nomad: a psychiatric problem. *Current Psychiatric Therapies 21*:253–61.

Aptekar, Lewis (1988). *Street children of Cali*. Durham, NC: Duke University Press.

Argeriou, Milton, and Dennis McCarty (Eds.) (1990). *Treating alcoholism and drug abuse among homeless men and women: Nine community demonstration grants*. New York: Haworth Press.

Asuni, T. (1968). Vagrant psychotics in Abeokuta. *Proc. deux. colloque africaine de psychiatrie*, 115–23. Paris: AUDECAM, as cited in Baasher et al., 1983.

Athanas, Diane (1991). Growing old: The invisibility of aging women in France. Paper presented at the annual meeting of the American Anthropological Association. Chicago.

Austerberry, Helen, and Sophie Watson (1983). *Women on the margins: A study of single women's housing problems*. London: Housing Research Group, The City University.

Baasher, T., et al. (1983). On vagrancy and psychosis. *Community Mental Health Journal 19*(1):27–41.

Bachrach, Leona L. (1980). Overview: Model programs for chronic mental patients. *American Journal of Psychiatry 137*(9):1023–31.

_____ (1984). Research on services for the homeless mentally ill. Conference report. *Hospital and Community Psychiatry 35*(9):910–13.

Back Wards to Back Streets (1980). Video recording. New York: Film Makers Library.

Bahr, Howard, and Gerald Garrett (1976). *Women alone: The disaffiliation of urban females*. Lexington, MA: Lexington Books.

Bannerjee, S. (1979). *Child labour in India*. Child Labour Series, no. 2. Anti-Slavery Society, London. Cited in P. M. Shah, Health status of working and street children and alternative approaches to their health care. *Advances in international maternal and child health 7* (1987):70–93.

_____ (1980). *Child labour in Thailand*. Child Labour Series, no. 4. Anti-Slavery Society, London. Cited in P. M. Shah, Health status of working and street children and alternative approaches to their health care. *Advances in international maternal and child health 7* (1987):70–93.

Barker, Gary Knaul (1991a). Evidence from around the world points to increasing violence against street children. *Esperanza 3* (June):1, 4.

_____ (1991b). Reaching the hard-to-reach: Health strategies for serving urban young women. *CHILDHOPE* USA Working Paper no. 2.

Barker, Gary, and Felicia Knaul (1991). *Exploited entrepreneurs: street and working children in developing countries*. New York: CHILDHOPE-USA.

_____ (1990). AIDS: A growing threat to street children. *Esperanza 2* (October):1, 6.

Bassuk, Ellen, Lenore Rubin, and Alison Lauriat (1986). Characteristics of sheltered homeless families. *American Journal of Public Health 76*(9):1097–1101.

Baxter, Ellen, and Kim Hopper (1981). Private lives/public spaces: Homeless adults on the streets of New York City. New York: Community Service Society.

Beard, Rick (Ed.) (1987). *On being homeless: Historical perspectives*. New York: Museum of the City of New York.

Bennet, James (1992). Leaving shelters for more uncertainty. *New York Times*. 16 July, pp. B1, B4.

Berck, Judith (1992). No place to be: voices of homeless children. *Public Welfare 50*(2) (Spring):28–33.

Bethell, Lauran Dale (1991). Personal communication with author regarding work with prostitutes in Thailand and Buram, some of whom are in danger of homelessness.

Boehi, Willi (1991). Report sent to author by Fr. Gottfried Vonwyl, SMB, of the Bettlehem Mission Society, Taiwan, 22 November.

Bohlen, Celestine (1990). Hungary's new burden: Army of homeless. *New York Times*. 23 October, pp. A1, A8.

Boudimbou, Guy (1992). Les immigrés africains et le squatt des logements sociaux dans la région parisienne. Paper presented at the Fifth International Research Conference on Housing, Montreal, Quebec, July 7–10. Translated by Charlotte Biederman.

Boyko, Ernie (1992). Director, Census Operations Division, Statistics Canada. Letter to author, 13 December.

Brandon, David (1974). *Homeless*. London: Sheldon Press.

Breton, Margot (1988). The need for mutual-aid groups in a drop-in for homeless women: The *Sistering* Case. *Social Work with Groups 11*(4):47–61.

Brickner P., et al. (1984). Medical aspects of the homeless. In H. R. Lamb (Ed.), *The homeless mentally ill*. Washington DC: American Psychiatric Association.

Bromley, Ray (1988). Working in the streets. In Josef Gugler (Ed.), *The Urbanization of the Third World* (pp. 161–82). Oxford: Oxford University Press.

Brokaw, Tom (1991). Exposé. *NBC News Magazine*. 10 February.

Bruns, Roger A. (1980). *Knights of the road: A hobo history*. New York: Methuen.

Bunston, Terry, and Margot Breton (1990). The eating patterns and problems of homeless women. *Women & Health 16*(1):43–62.

Burt, Martha R., and Barbara E. Cohen (1989). Differences among homeless single women, women with children, and single men. *Social Problems 36*(5):508–24.

Butler, Anne M. (1985). *Daughters of joy, sisters of misery: Prostitutes in the American West, 1865–90*. Urbana: University of Illinois Press.

Canter, David (1988). Homelessness in west central London: Preliminary report on experimental pilot count of people who are homeless in west central London. Guildford: University of Surrey.

Caplow, Theodore, Howard M. Bahr, and David Sternberg (1968). Homelessness. In David L. Sills (Ed.), *International Encyclopedia of the Social Sciences* (vol. 6, pp. 494–98). New York: Free Press.

Carvel, John (1990). Destitute teenagers face jail penalty. *The Guardian*. 3 January, p. 4.

Chavkin W., et al. (1987). Reproductive experience of women living in hotels for the homeless in New York City. *New York State Journal of Medicine 87*:10–13.

Chez Doris (1992). Informational packet for volunteers. Montreal.

CHILDHOPE (1987). *Our child our hope. Journal of the International Movement on Behalf of Street Children 1*(2).

Child Workers in Nepal Concerned Center (1990). *Lost childhood: A survey of research on the street children of Kathmandu.* Kathmandu, Nepal: CWIN.

Children's Defense Fund (1988). *A children's defense budget FY 1989; An analysis of our nation's investment in children.* Washington DC: Children's Defense Fund.

Cohen, Carol I., and Jay Sokolovsky (1989). *Old men of the Bowery: Strategies for survival among the homeless.* New York: Guilford Press.

Cole, John (1987). *Development and underdevelopment: A profile of the Third World.* London: Methuen.

Coleman, John R. (1986). Diary of a homeless man. In Jon Erickson and Charles Wilhelm (Eds.), *Housing the homeless* (pp. 37–52). New Brunswick, NJ: Center for Urban Policy Research.

Connolly, Mark (1990). Adrift in the city: A comparative study of street children in Bogotá, Colombia, and Guatemala City. In Nancy A. Boxill (Ed.), *Homeless children: The watchers and the waiters* (pp. 129–49). New York: Haworth Press.

Conroy, J. D. (1987). *Shelter for the homeless: Asian-Pacific needs and Australian responses.* Development Dossier, no. 22. Washington, DC: Federal Department of Housing and Construction.

Cornia, Giovanni Andrea, and Sandor Sipos (Eds.) (1991). *Children and the transition to the market economy: Safety nets and social policies in Central and Eastern Europe.* Aldershot, England: Avebury.

Crossette, Barbara (1990). Homeless and hungry youths of India. *New York Times.* International Sunday, 23 December.

Curcio, William (1992). Mediation and homelessness. *Public Welfare 50*(2): 34–39.

Dallape, Fabio (1991). Beginning with street children. *Together: A Journal of World Vision International 32* (October–December):8–10.

Daly, Gerald (1990a). Health implications of homelessness: Reports from three countries. *Journal of Sociology and Social Welfare 27*(1):111–25.

_____ (1990b). Programs dealing with homelessness in the United States, Canada and Britain. In Jamshid Momeni (Ed.), *Homelessness in the United States: Data and issues.* New York: Praeger.

Das, Bidyut K. (1986) *The rural poor in the city: A study on social transformation among the pavement dwellers in Calcutta.* Calcutta: Anthropological Survey of India, Government of India.

_____ (n.d.). *Migration and social change: A study of pavement dwellers in Calcutta.* Anthropological Survey of India, Government of India.

Day, Marie (1992). Author visit to Chez Doris, 23 April, Montreal, Quebec.

De Jesus, Carolina Maria (1963). *Child of the dark: The diary of Carolina Maria De Jesus.* Translated from the Portuguese. New York: New American Library.

de la Puente, Manuel (1990). The census undercount of the Hispanic population. *A staff working paper: Undercount behavioral research group*. Washington DC: Bureau of the Census.

DeParle, Jason (1992a). Rescuing drunks from the cold and swapping war stories. *New York Times*. 24 September, p. B12.

_____ (1992b). "Safety Net" has ended days when homeless froze to death in Anchorage. *New York Times*. 24 September, p. B12.

Der Spiegel (1992). Das ist legale Vertreibung (Hannah Clements, Trans.). *Der Spiegel 46*:76–92.

Dogan, Mattei, and John D. Kasarda (Eds.) (1988). *A world of giant cities: The metropolis era*, vol. 1. Newbury Park, CA: Sage Publications.

_____ (1988). *Mega-cities: The metropolis era*, vol. 2. Newbury Park, CA: Sage Publications.

Drakakis-Smith, David (1987). *The Third World city*. London: Methuen.

Dugger, Celia W. (1992a). Big shelters hold terrors for the mentally ill. *New York Times*. 12 January, pp. 1, 22.

_____ (1992b). Memo to Democrats: Housing won't solve homelessness. *New York Times*. 12 July, p. E9.

_____ (1992c). Threat only when on crack, homeless man foils system. *New York Times*. 3 September, pp. A1, B4.

Ember, Carol R., and Melvin Ember (1990). *Anthropology*. 6th ed. Englewood Cliffs, NJ: Prentice-Hall.

Ennew, Judith (1986). Children of the street. *New Internationalist*:10–11.

Ennew, Judith, and Brian Milne (1990). *The next generation: Lives of Third World children*. Philadelphia: New Society Publishers.

Eyre,L. Alan (1990). The shanty towns of Central Bombay. *Urban Geography 11*(2):130–52.

Fabrega, Horacio Jr. (1971). Begging in a southeastern Mexican city. *Human Organization 303*:277–87.

Fallis, George, and Alex Murray (Eds.) (1990). *Housing the homeless and poor*. Toronto: University of Toronto Press.

Felsman, Kirk (1981). Street urchins of Colombia. *Natural History 90*(4):40–49.

Fennell, Dodee (1974). Uncommon people (unpublished paper). Cited in Marsha A. Martin, Homeless women: An historical perspective. In Rick Beard (Ed.), *On being homeless: Historical perspectives*. New York: Museum of the City of New York, 1987, 37.

Ferrand-Bechmann, Dan (1988). Homeless in France: Public and private policies. In Jürgen Friedrichs (Ed.), *Affordable housing and the homeless* (pp. 147–55). Berlin: Walter de Gruyter.

_____ (1990). Très pauvre et très mal logé: L'action des grandes associations face à l'extrême pauvreté. In Dan Ferrand-Bechmann (Ed.), *Pauvre et mal logé: Les enjeux sociaux de l'habitat* (pp. 71–86). Trans. Charlotte Biederman. Paris: Éditions L'Harmattan.

Finnegan, Frances (1979). *Poverty and prostitution: A study of Victorian prostitutes in York*. Cambridge: Cambridge University Press.

Fischer, Pamela J., and William R. Breakey (1986). Homelessness and mental health. *International Journal of Mental Health 14*(4):6–41.

Fitchen, Janet M. (1991). *Endangered spaces, enduring places: Change, identity and survival in rural America*. Boulder: Westview.

_____ (1981). *Poverty in Rural America: A Case Study*. Boulder: Westview.

Fonseca, Claudia (1986). Orphanages, foundlings, and foster mothers: The system of child circulation in a Brazilian squatter settlement. *Anthropological Quarterly 1*(59):15–27.

Friedrichs, Jürgen (Ed.) (1988). *Affordable housing and the homeless*. Berlin: Walter de Gruyter.

Gandotra, S. R. (1977). *Census of India: Special study— houseless in Delhi*. New Delhi, India: Director of Census Operations.

Gelberg, Lillian, and Lawrence Linn (1989). Assessing the physical health of homeless adults. *Journal of the American Medical Association 262*(14):1973–79.

George, Dorothy (1965). *London life in the 18th century*. New York: Capricorn Books.

Giel R., et al. (1974). Ticket to heaven: Psychiatric illness in a religious community in Ethiopia. *Social Science and Medicine 8*(8):549–56.

Gillin, J. L. (1929). Vagrancy and begging. *American Journal of Sociology 35*(35):424–32.

Gilmore, Harlan W. (1940). *The beggar*. Chapel Hill: University of North Carolina Press.

Glass, Ruth (1964). *London: Aspects of change*. London: Centre for Urban Studies and MacGillion & Kee. In George A. Thomas, The gentrification of paradise: St. John's Antigua. *Urban Geography 12*(5) (1991):469–87.

Glasser, Irene (1991). An ethnographic study of homeless in Windham, Connecticut. Report no. 17. Washington DC: Ethnographic Exploratory Research, Center for Survey Methods Research, Bureau of the Census.

_____ (1988). *More than bread: Ethnography of a soup kitchen*. Tuscaloosa: University of Alabama Press.

_____ (1992a). Emergency food programs and the homeless. Paper read at the American Anthropological Association Annual Meetings, San Francisco, CA.

_____ (1992b). Visit to Chez Doris, Montreal, Quebec, 23 April.

Golden, Stephanie (1992). *The women outside*. Berkeley: University of California Press.

Goldman, Brian (1988). Health of Toronto's street kids disturbing, study reveals. *Canadian Medical Association Journal 138*:1041–43.

Gonzalez, David (1992). For some, shelters mean chaos and home. *New York Times*. 17 July, pp. B1–B2.

Goodman, Lisa A. (1991). The prevalence of abuse among homeless and housed poor mothers: A comparison study. *American Journal of Orthopsychiatry* 6(14):489–500.

Gostin, Lawrence O. (1993). Controlling the resurgent tuberculosis epidemic. *JAMA: The Journal of the American Medical Association 269*(2):255–61.

Gugler, Josef (Ed.) (1988). *The urbanization of the Third World*. Oxford: Oxford University Press.

Gumpel, Andrew (1992). Homelessness straining fabric of life in Paris. *Sun Sentinel*. 27 February, p. 7A.

Guo, Zibin (1992). Telephone call to author, 10 July, from anthropologist in the United States.

Gutiérrez, José (1972a). *Gamin: Un ser Olvidado*. Mexico City: Libros McGraw-Hill.

_____ (1972b). The gamines. In Jules H. Masserman (Ed.), *Science and psychoanalysis: research and relevance* (vol. 21, pp. 45–60). New York: Grune & Stratton.

_____ (1970). Using a clinical methodology in a social study of deviant children. *Case Western Reserve Journal of Sociology IV* (December):1–28.

Habitat International Coalition (1992). *HIC News* No. 9, vol. 3, no. 3.

Hagen, Jan L., and Andre M. Ivanoff (1988). Homeless women: A high -risk population. *Affilia: Journal of Women and Social Work 3*(1):19–33.

Hand, Jennifer (1984). *Shopping bag ladies*. Ph.D. dissertation, New School for Social Research, New York. Cited in Marsha A. Martin, Homeless women: An historical perspective. In Rick Beard (Ed.), *On being homeless: Historical perspectives*. New York: Museum of the City of New York, 1987, 37.

Hardoy, Jorge E., and David Satterthwaite (1981). *Shelter: Need and response: Housing, land and settlement policies in seventeen Third World nations*. Chicester, England: Wiley.

_____ (1989). *Squatter citizen: Life in the urban Third World*. London: Earthscan Publications.

Hauch, Christopher (1985). *Coping strategies and street life: The ethnography of Winnipeg's skid row*. Region Report no. 11. Winnipeg: Institute of Urban Studies.

Hester, Jeffrey T. (1991). Yoseba: Day laborers' communities of urban Japan. *Working Papers in Asian/Pacific Studies*:91–02. Durham, NC: Asian/Pacific Studies Institute, Duke University.

_____ (1993). Telephone call to author, 8 January.

Hill, Ronald Paul (1991). Health care and the homeless: A marketing-oriented approach. *Journal of Health Care Marketing 11*:14–23.

Holch, C., and R. A. Slayton (1989). *New homeless and old: Community and the skid row hotel.* Philadelphia: Temple University Press.

Hollnsteiner, Mary Racelis, and Peter Taçon (1983). Urban migration in developing countries: Consequences for their families and children. In Daniel A. Wagner (Ed.), *Child development and international development: Research-policy interfaces* (pp. 5–26). San Francisco: Jossey-Bass.

Homelessness in industrialised countries (1987). Report by the International Federation for Housing and Planning (IFHP). Netherlands.

Hulchanski, J. David, et al. (1991). *Solutions to homelessness: Vancouver Case Studies.* Vancouver: University of British Columbia.

Hunt, Kathleen (1991). The Romanian baby bazaar. *The New York Times Magazine.* 24 March, pp. 24–29, 38, 53.

Hutson, Susan (1993). Letter to author, 28 January.

——— (1992). Letter to author, 1 January.

Huttman, Elizabeth (1988). Homelessness as a housing problem in an inner city in the U.S. In Jürgen Friedrichs (Ed.), *Affordable housing and the homeless* (pp. 157–74). Berlin: Walter de Gruyter.

Inside life outside (1988). Video recording. New York: West Glenn Films.

Institute of Medicine (1988). *Homelessness, health, and human needs committee on health care for homeless people.* Washington, DC: National Academy Press.

International Catholic Child Bureau (1991). *The sexual exploitation of children: Field responses.* Geneva: International Catholic Child Bureau (Florence Bruce, project coordinator).

International Labour Office (1980). *A bureau of statistics and special studies.* Geneva: International Labour Office. Cited in P. M. Shah, Health status of working and street children and alternative approaches to their health care. *Advances in international maternal and child health 7* (1987):70–93.

Inter-NGO Programme on Street Children and Street Youth (1983). Summary of Proceedings. Cited in P. M. Shah, Health status of working and street children and alternative approaches to their health care. *Advances in international maternal and child health 7* (1987):70–93.

Irvine, Graeme (1991). Abandoned children: the most marginalized. *Together: A Journal of World Vision International 32* (October–December):1–2.

Jansen, Willy (1987). *Women without men: Gender and marginality in an Algerian town.* Netherlands: E. J. Brill.

Jones, Paul (1991). Ministering to street children. *Together: A Journal of World Vision International 32* (October–December):3–5.

Joseph Rowntree Foundation (1991). Temporary housing for homeless people. Housing Research Findings, no. 50. York, England: Joseph Rountree Foundation.

Justin, Renate (1987). Glue: The street child's escape. *Our Child Our Hope, Journal of the International Movement on Behalf of Street Children 1*(2):4.

Kalff, Elsbeth (1990). Les chiffonniers de Paris: Dans les "Bidonvilles" du XIX Siècle (1820–1920). In Dan Ferrand-Bechmann (Ed.), *Pauvre et Mal Logé: Les enjeux sociaux de l'habitat* (pp. 17–34). Trans. Charlotte Biederman. Paris: Éditions L'Harmattan.

Kalifon, S. Zev (1989). Homelessness and mental illness: Who resorts to the state hospital? *Human Organization 48*(3):268–79.

Keare, Douglas H., and Scott Parris (1982). *Evaluation of shelter programs of the urban poor: Principal findings.* World Bank Staff Working Papers, no. 547. Washington DC: The World Bank.

Kozol, Jonathan (1988). *Rachel and her children.* New York: Crown.

Kudryavtse, E. (1986). *I hereby apply for an apartment.* Moscow: Progress Publishers.

Kylmala, Jouni (1991). Two perspectives to the life of skid row alcoholics: Adaptation and distinction. In Juhani Lehto (Ed.), *Deprivation, social welfare and expertise.* Research Reports. Helsinki, Finland: National Agency for Welfare and Health.

Labeodan, Olusola Adebola (1989). The Homeless in Ibadan. *Habitat International 13*(1):75–85.

Lamb, H. Richard (1984). Deinstitutionalization and the homeless mentally ill. *Hospital and Community Psychiatry 35*(9):899–907.

———— (1979). The new asylums in the community. *Archives of General Psychiatry 36*:129–34.

Langergaard, Af Jens (1992). Hjemloxe bliver ladt I stikken. Trans. Solvej Jensen. *Dit Fri Aktuelt.* 6 January, pp. 2, 3.

Levine, Robert M. (1992). The cautionary tale of Carolina Maria De Jesus. Working Paper, no. 178. Notre Dame, IN: Kellogg Institute, University of Notre Dame.

Levinson, David (1974). Skid row in transition. *Urban Anthropology 3*(1):79–93.

Liddiard, Mark, and Susan Hutson (1991a). Homeless young people and run-aways—agency definitions and processes. *Journal of Social Policy 20*(3):365–88.

———— (1991b). Young and Homeless in Wales. Monograph No. 26. In Hans Kroes and John Lane (Eds.), *Homelessness in industrialised countries.* Report by the International Federation for Housing and Planning (IFHP) Standing Committee "Housing." Netherlands.

Liegeois, Jean-Pierre (1986). *Gypsies: An illustrated history.* Worcester, England: Billing. Orig. pub. as *Tsiganes.* Paris: La Découverte, 1983.

———— 1987. *Gypsies and travellers.* Strasbourg, France: Council of Europe.

Lomax, Alan (1975). *The folk songs of North America.* Garden City, NY: Dolphin Books.

Lozada, Rebecca (n.d.). No harbor: The children around Subic Naval Base. *Simbayan*:17–19.

Lubeck, Paul M. (1981). Islamic networks and urban capitalism: An instance of articulation from Northern Nigeria. *Cahiers d'études africaines* 21(1–3):67–78.

Ludder, Elisabeth, et al. (1990). Health and nutrition survey in a group of urban homeless adults. *Journal of the American Dietetic Association* 90(10):1387–92

Mahood, Linda (1990). *The Magdalenes: Prostitution in the nineteenth century.* London: Routledge.

Mahmoud, Adele M. (1982). Schistosomiasis. In James B. Wyngaarden and Lloyd H. Smith, Jr. (Eds.), *Cecil textbook of medicine* (pp. 1754–60). Philadelphia: Saunders Company.

Marin, Peter (1991). The prejudice against men. *Nation* (8 July):46–51.

Martin, Elizabeth (1992). Assessment of S-Night street enumeration in the 1990 census. *Evaluation Review* 16(4):418–38.

Martin, Marsha A. (1987). Homeless women: An historical perspective. In Rick Beard (Ed.), *On being homeless: Historical perspectives* (pp. 33–42). New York: Museum of the City of New York.

Martin, Marsha A., and Susan A. Nayowith (1988). Creating community: Group work to develop social support networks with homeless mentally ill. *Social Work with Groups* 11(4):79–93.

Maxwell, Carol J. C. (1991). The causes and character of Gaminismo: Street children in Colombia. Unpublished manuscript.

Mayhew, Henry (1968). *London labour and the London poor: A cyclopaedia of the condition and earnings of those that will work, those that cannot work, and those that will not work 1861–1862.* 4 vols. New York: Dover.

McAuslan, Patrick (1985). *Urban land and shelter for the poor.* London and Washington, DC: Earthscan International Institute for Environment and Development.

McCann, Wendy (1992). Street City, une solution au problème des sans-abri. Trans. Charlotte Biederman. *La Presse.* Sent to author, 11 January.

McElroy, Ann, and Patricia K. Townsend (1989). *Medical anthropology in ecological perspective.* Boulder: Westview.

Milburn, Norweeta, and Ann D'Ercole (Eds.) (1991). Homeless women, children, and families. *American Psychologist* 46(11) (November):1159–1218.

Miller, Henry (1991). *On the fringe: The dispossessed in America.* Lexington, MA: Lexington Books.

Mills, Heather (1990). Street couple resigned to a life without hope. *The Independent* (London). Sent to author, 8 January.

Miskura, Susan M. (1989). The enumeration of doubled-up families. 1990 Decennial Census Policy Memorandum No. 22. Washington DC: Bureau of the Census, United States Department of Commerce.

Mitchell, J. Clyde (1987). The components of strong ties among homeless women. *Social Networks* 9:37–47.

Momeni, J. A. (Ed.) (1989). *Homelessness in the United States. Vol. 1: State Surveys*. New York: Greenwood Press.

Moore, Jeanne, et al. (1991). The faces of homelessness. Guildford: Housing Research Unit, University of Surrey.

Morgan, Thomas (1992). Homeless put into hotels for tourists. *New York Times*. 28 August, pp. B1–B2.

Moser, Caroline O. N., and Linda Peake (Eds.) (1987). *Women, human settlements, and housing*. London: Tavistock.

Morse, Gary A., Robert J. Calsyn, and Gery K. Burger (1991). A comparison of taxonomic systems for classifying homeless men. *The International Journal of Social Psychiatry 37*(2):90–98.

Muñoz, V. C., and X. C. Pachón (1980). *Gamines testimonios*. Bogotá, Colombia: Carlos Valencia Editores. Cited in Lewis Aptekar, *Street children of Cali*. Durham, NC: Duke University Press, 1988.

Murie, Alan (Ed.) (1987). *Living in a bed and breakfast: The experience of homelessness in London*. Bristol: School for Advanced Urban Studies, University of Bristol.

Murie, Alan, and Ray Forrest (1988). The new homeless in Britain. In Jürgen Friedrichs (Ed.), *Affordable Housing and the Homeless* (pp. 129–45). Berlin: Walter de Gruyter.

Murison, Hamish S., and John P. Lea (Eds.) (1979). *Housing in Third World countries: Perspectives on policy and practice*. New York: St. Martin's.

Murray, Alison, J. (1991). *No money, no honey: A study of street traders and prostitutes in Jakarta*. Singapore: Oxford University Press.

Murray, Harry (1986). Time in the streets. In Jon Erickson and Charles Wilhelm (Eds.), *Housing the Homeless* (pp. 53–69). New Brunswick, NJ: Center for Urban Policy Research.

My sky, my home (1990). Video recording. Honolulu: East/West Center.

Nanda, Serena (1991). *Cultural anthropology*. Belmont, CA: Wadsworth.

Nash, Nathaniel (1991). Youths trampled in Peru's gold rush. *New York Times*. 26 August, p. A8.

National Campaign for Housing Rights (1991). Housing rights in the 1991 election manifestos. Calcutta: NCHR Campaign Clearinghouse.

Navarro, Mireya (1992). Pill monitors make sure TB patients swallow. *New York Times*. 5 September, pp. 1, 22.

Neil, Cecily, and Rodney Fopp (1992). Homelessness in Australia (Draft). Melbourne: Ministerial Advisory Committee on Homelessness and Housing.

Nelson, Marcia Z. (1986). Street people. In Jon Erickson and Charles Wilhelm (Eds.), *Housing the homeless* (pp. 17–25). New Brunswick, NJ: Center for Urban Policy Research.

New York Times (1992). Bill Clinton. Editorial, 1 November, p. 16.

Noble, Kenneth B. (1991). Nigeria, its borders sealed, sends 700,000 workers to take census. *New York Times*. 29 November, pp. A1, A15.

Novick, Robert E. (1987). Shelter and health. *World Health* (July): 6–9.

Ng, Peter (1991). Personal communication regarding Indonesian term for homelessness, received through electronic mail, South Asia Discussion Group, 25 October.

Oberlander, H. Peter, and Arthur L. Fallick (1987). *Shelter or homes? A contribution to the search for solutions to homelessness in Canada*. Vancouver: The Centre for Human Settlements, University of British Columbia.

O'Brien, Anne (1988). *Poverty's prison: The poor in New South Wales 1889–1918*. Carlton, Australia: Melbourne University Press.

O'Brien, Patricia (1973). *The woman alone*. New York: Quadrangle.

Ohya, Marie (1992). Interview with author, 19 April.

Ojanuga, Durrenda Nash (1990). Kaduna beggar children: A study of child abuse and neglect in Northern Nigeria. *Child Welfare LXIX*(4):371–80.

Okely, Judith (1983). *The Traveller-Gypsies*. Cambridge: Cambridge University Press.

Oliver, Paul (1987). *Dwellings: The house across the world*. Austin: University of Texas Press.

Ontario Task Force on Roomers, Boarders and Lodgers (1986). *A place to call home: Housing solutions for low-income singles in Ontario*. Toronto: Ontario Ministry of Housing. As cited in Hulchanski, et al. (1991). *Solutions to homelessness: Vancouver case studies*. Vancouver: University of British Columbia.

Oram, Nigel (1979). Housing, planning and urban administration. In Hamish S. Murison and John P. Lea (Eds.), *Housing in Third World countries: Perspectives on policy and practice*. New York: St. Martin's.

Orwell, George (1933). *Down and out in Paris and London*. San Diego: Harcourt Brace.

Payne, Geoffrey (1989). *Informal housing and land subdivisions in Third World cities: A review of the literature*. Oxford, England: Overseas Development Administration (ODA), the Centre for Development and Environmental Planning (CENDEP), at Oxford Polytechnic.

Pearce, Diana M. (1988). The invisible homeless: Women and children. Washington, DC: Locked Out: Women and Housing. Women's Research and Education Institute, Institute for Women's Policy Research.

Peters, Lisa (1987). Images of the homeless in American art, 1860–1919. In Rick Beard (Ed.), *On being homeless: Historical perspectives* (pp. 43–67). New York: Museum of the City of New York.

Phongpalchit, Pasuk (1982). *From peasant girls to Bangkok masseuses*. Geneva: International Labour Organisation.

Piven, Frances Fox, and Richard A. Cloward (1971). *Regulating the poor: The functions of public welfare*. New York: Pantheon.

Pixote (1981). Video recording. Burbank, CA: Embrafilms.

Priest, R. G. (1976). The homeless person and the psychiatric services: An Edinburgh survey. *British Journal of Psychiatry 128.* As cited in Fischer and Breakey (1986). Homelessness and mental health. *International Journal of Mental Health 14*(4):6–41.

Pye, Lucian W. (1991): The state and the individual: An overview interpretation. *China Quarterly,* no. 127: 443–66.

Rafferty, Margaret, et al. (1984). *The shelter worker's handbook.* A Project by the Health Committee of the Coalition for the Homeless.

Rafferty, Yvonne, and Marybeth Shinn (1991). The impact of homelessness on children. *American Psychologist 46*(11) (November):1170–79.

Ramchandaran, P. (1972). *Pavement dwellers in Bombay City.* Series no. 26. Bombay: Tata Institute of Social Science.

Ranschburg, Jeno (1990). Current situation of families and children in Hungary. Mimeograph. UNICEF/ICDC. Florence: International Child Development Centre. As cited in Giovanni Andrea Cornia and Sandor Sipos (Eds.), *Children and the Transition to the Market Economy Safety Nets and Social Policies in Central and Eastern Europe* (pp. 11–31). Aldershot, Eng.: Avebury, 1991.

Redick R., and M. Witkin (1983). *State and county mental hospitals, U.S. 1970–1980 and 1980–1981 Mental Health Statistical Note 169.* Rockville, MD: National Institute of Mental Health.

Reitman, Ben L. (1937/1975). *Sister of the road: The autobiography of Box-Car Bertha, as told to Dr. Ben L. Reitman.* New York: Harper & Row.

Rivlin, Leanne (1990). Home and homelessness in the lives of children. In Nancy A. Boxill (Ed.), *Homeless children: The watchers and the waiters* (pp. 129–49). New York: Haworth Press.

Roa, N. Rama (1992). Letter to the author from Deputy Registrar General, Office of the Registrar General, India, 18 March.

Robbins, Tom (1986). New York's homeless families. In Jon Erickson and Charles Wilhelm (Eds.), *Housing the homeless* (pp. 26–36). New Brunswick, NJ: Center for Urban Policy Research.

Robertson, Marjorie J. (1991). Homeless women with children: The role of alcohol and other drug abuse. *American Psychologist 46*(11):1198–04.

Rocky, M. (1989). Testimony before the Senate Committee on Appropriations, Subcommittee on Foreign Operations. CHILDHOPE. New York, 11 July. In Barker and Knaul, Reaching the hard-to reach: Health strategies for serving urban young women. CHILDHOPE USA Working Paper no. 2.

Room, Robin (1984). Alcohol and ethnography: A case of deflation. *Current Anthropology 25*:2. In Jouni Kylmala (1991), Two perspectives to the life of skid row alcoholics: Adaptation and distinction. In Juhani Lehto (Ed.), *Deprivation, social welfare and expertise.* Research Reports. Finland: National Agency for Welfare and Health.

Ropers, Richard (1988). *The invisible homeless: A new urban ecology*. New York: Insight Books, Human Science Press.

Rossi, P. (1989). *Down and out in America: The origins of homelessness*. Chicago: University of Chicago Press.

Rotheram-Borus, Mary Jane, Cheryl Koopman, and Anke A. Ehrhardt (1991). Homeless youths and HIV infection. *American Psychologist 46*(11):1188–97.

Rousseau, Ann Marie (1981). *Shopping bag ladies*. New York: Pilgrim Press.

Rowe, Stacy, and Jennifer Wolch (1990). Social networks in time and space: Homeless women in skid row, Los Angeles. *Annals of the Association of American Geographers 80*(2):184–204.

Salaam Bombay (1986). Video recording. Chatsworth, CA: Image Entertainment.

Salo, Mikko (1988). Personal interview in Connecticut with Professor Salo of the University of Joensu, Joensu, Finland, 22 April.

Sanders, Thomas G. (1987). Brazilian street children: Part I: Who they are. *UFSI* Reports. Indianapolis: Universities Field Staff International.

Sarin, Madhu (1980). *Policies towards urban slums: Slums and squatter settlements in the ESCAP region: Case studies of seven cities*. United Nations. Bangkok: Housing, Building and Planning Section, Economic and social commission for Asia and the Pacific (ESCAP).

Schaefer, Morris (1987). Health principles of housing. *World Health* (July): 18–19.

Schenk, John (1991). From "parking boy" to drug counselor. *Together: A Journal of World Vision International 32* (October–December):10–11.

Schmidt, William E. (1992). Across Europe, faces of homeless become more visible and vexing. *New York Times*. 5 January, pp. 1, 8.

Settlements Information Network Africa (SINA) (1986a). Case study on Undugu society squatter upgrading in Nairobi. Nairobi: Mazingira Institute.

_____ (1986b). *NGOs and shelter*. Fifteen case studies from Africa on housing and shelter programs. Articles from Angola, Botswana, Ghana, Kenya, Malawi, Mozambique, Nigeria, Tanzania, and Zimbabwe. Nairobi: Mazingira Institute.

Shah, P. M. (1987). Health status of working and street children and alternative approaches to their health care. *Advances in International Maternal and Child Health 7*:70–93.

Shinn, Marybeth, James R. Knickman, and Beth C. Weitzman (1991). Social relationships and vulnerability to becoming homeless among poor families. *American Psychologist 46*(11):1180–87.

Shostak, Marjorie (1983). *Nisa*. New York: Vintage Books.

Shulsinger, Esther (1990). Needs of sheltered homeless children. *Journal of Pediatric Health Care 4*(3):136–40.

Situationer on rural to urban migration (1990). Paper sent to author from

Research Committee of the National Council of Social Development Foundation of the Philippines, Inc.

Sjamsir, Sjarif (1991). Personal communication regarding Indonesian term for homelessness, received through electronic mail, South Asia Discussion Group, 25 October.

Smith, Joan, and Sheila Gilford (1991). Homelessness among under-25's. *Findings*. York, England: Joseph Rowntree Foundation.

Soliman, Ahmed M. (1992). Housing consolidation and the urban poor: the case of Hagar el Nawateyah, Alexandria. *Environment and Urbanization* 4(2):184–95.

Spradley, James (1970). *You owe yourself a drunk: An ethnography of urban nomads*. Boston: Little, Brown.

Srivastava, S. C. (1983). *Indian census in perspective*. New Delhi: Office of the Registrar General, Ministry of Home Affairs.

Statistics Canada (n.d.a). 1991 Canadian census of population enumeration in shelters and soup kitchens. Ottawa: Statistics Canada.

_____ (n.d.b). 1991 census form SK-4: Interviewer reference guide and reasons why questions are asked. Ottawa: Statistics Canada.

Streetwise (1988). Video recording. Los Angeles: New World Video.

Stoner, Madeleine R. (1983). The plight of homeless women. *Social Service Review* 57(4):565–81.

Summa, Hilkka (1991). The homeless as an object of administrative discourse. In Juhani Lehto (Ed.), *Deprivation, social welfare and expertise*. Research Reports. Helsinki: National Agency for Welfare and Health.

Suri, Sonia (1993). Telephone conversation with author, 20 August.

Suroviak, Jane (1993). Author visit with director, Thames River Valley Family Program, Norwich, Connecticut, 8 January.

Sway, Marlene (1988). *Familiar strangers: Gypsy life in America*. Urbana: University of Illinois Press.

Taçon, Peter (1986). Carlinhos: The hard gloss of city polish. *UNICEF News* 111(11):4–5.

_____ (1984a). I know my father's here somewhere. *Ideas Forum*. UNICEF (18):5.

_____ (1984b). Is one in four called "winning"? *Ideas Forum*. UNICEF (18):2.

Taeuber, Cynthia, and Paul M. Siegel (1990). Counting the Nation's homeless population in the 1990 census. Washington, DC: Bureau of the Census, U.S. Department of Commerce.

Taipale, Ilkka (1979). Terms applied to deviant drinkers in Finland. *Reports from the Social Institute of Alcohol Studies 134*. In Jouni Kylmala (1991), Two perspectives to the life of skid row alcoholics: Adaptation and distinction. In Juhani Lehto (Ed.), *Deprivation, social welfare and expertise*. Research Reports. Helsinki: National Agency for Welfare and Health.

Taylor, Paul (1987). Popular technology beats schisto. *World Health* (July):28–29.

Terrill, Ross (1991). Hong Kong. *National Geographic 179*(2):103–38.

Terry, Don (1992). Homeless prefer huts to Chicago's public housing. *New York Times.* 13 June, p. 7.

Thames River Family Program in Norwich, Connecticut (1992). Agency referral forms.

Thomas, Gerald. A. (1991). The gentrification of paradise: St. John's, Antigua. *Urban Geography 12*(5):469–87.

Thomas, Keith (1971). *Religion and the decline of magic.* New York: Scribner's.

Toronto Star (1989). Shelters leave families out in the cold. 22 December, p. 1. In Marlene Webber (1991), *Street kids: The tragedy of Canada's runaways* (p. 139). Toronto: University of Toronto Press.

Torrey, E. F. (1988). *Nowhere to go: The tragic odyssey of the homeless mentally ill.* New York: Harper and Row.

Trattner, Walter I. (1987). *From poor law to welfare state: A history of social welfare in America.* 4th ed. New York: Free Press.

Turner, Bertha (Ed.) (1988). *Building community: A Third World case book.* A summary of the Habitat International Coalition Non-Governmental Organization's Project for the International Year of Shelter for the Homeless, 1987, in association with Habitat Forum Berlin.

Turner, John (1976). *Housing by people: Towards autonomy in building environments.* London: Marion Boyars.

Turpijn, Wouter (1988). Shadow-housing self-help of dwellers in the Netherlands. In Jürgen Friedrichs (Ed.) (1988), *Affordable housing and the homeless* (pp. 103–13). Berlin: Walter de Gruyter.

Tyler, Stephen A. (1973). *India: An anthropological perspective.* Prospect Heights, IL: Waveland Press.

UNICEF (1986). Executive Board, 1986 session: Exploitation of working children and street children. In Barker and Knaul (1991), *Exploited entrepreneurs: Street and working children in developing countries* (p. 2). New York: CHILDHOPE-USA.

United Nations Centre for Human Settlements (1986). *Bulletin of the International Year of Shelter for the Homeless,* no. 6 (August). In Willem Van Vliet (1988), *Women, housing and community* (pp. 201–04). Aldershot, England: Avebury.

_____ (1990). *Shelter: From projects to national strategies.* International Year of Shelter for the Homeless.

United Nations (1983). *Demographic Yearbook 1981.* New York.

_____ (1989). *Demographic Yearbook 1987.* New York.

_____ (1991). *Demographic Yearbook 1989.* New York.

_____ (1992). *Demographic Yearbook 1990.* New York.

U.S. Department of Commerce, Bureau of the Census (1990a). Fact sheet for 1990 decennial census counts of persons in selected locations where homeless persons are found. Washington DC: Bureau of the Census.

———— (1990b). Summary of 1990 census plans for enumeration of the homeless. Washington DC: Bureau of the Census.

———— (1992). *Statistical abstract of the United States*. Washington DC: Bureau of the Census.

Van Vliet, Willem (Ed.) (1988). *Women, housing and community*. Aldershot, England: Avebury.

Vesanen, Pirjo (1991). On homelessness in Finland. Helsinki: National Agency for Welfare and Health.

Vesey-Fitzgerald, B. (1973). *Gypsies of Britain*. Rev. and enl. Orig. publ. 1944. Newton Abbot: David and Charles. As cited in Judith Okely, *The Traveller-Gypsies*. Cambridge: Cambridge University Press (pp. 1–37), 1983.

Voice of Child Workers (1990). Newsletter of Child Workers in Nepal Concerned Center (CWIN). Issue No. 9. Kathmandu, Nepal.

Wallace, S. E. (1965). *Skid row as a way of life*. Totawa, NJ: Bedminister.

Ward, J. (1989). *Organizing for the homeless*. Ottawa: Ottawa/Montreal Canadian Council on Social Development.

Ward, Peter (Ed.) (1982). *Self-help housing: A critique*. London: Mansell.

Ward, Victoria (1987). Street girls: The most vulnerable of street kids. Our Child Our Hope, Journal of the International Movement on Behalf of Street Children. *CHILDHOPE 1*(2):1, 10.

Watson, Sophie, and Helen Austerberry (1986). *Housing and homelessness: A feminist perspective*. London: Routledge & Kegan Paul.

Webber, Marlene (1991). *Street kids: The tragedy of Canada's runaways*. Toronto: University of Toronto Press.

Weisman, Steven R. (1991). Japan's homeless: Seen yet ignored. *New York Times*. International Saturday, 19 January, p. 4.

Wiseman, Jacqueline (1970). *Stations of the lost*. Chicago: University of Chicago Press. Rpt. 1979.

Wolch, Jennifer (1990). Homelessness in America: A review of recent books. *Journal of Urban Affairs 12*(4):449–63.

Women's Institute for Housing and Economic Development, Inc. (1986). *A manual on transitional housing*. Boston.

World Vision International (1991). *Together: A Journal of World Vision International 32* (October–December). Issue devoted to abandoned children.

Wren, Christopher S. (1991). Mean streets swallow the orphans of apartheid. *New York Times*. 10 December, p. A4.

Wresinski, J. (1987). Grande pauvreté et précarité économique et sociale. *Journal Officiel*. 11–12 February. Paris: 26, rue Desaix. In Dan Ferrand-Bechmann (1988), Homeless in France: Public and private policies. In

Jürgen Friedrichs (Ed.), *Affordable housing and the homeless.* Berlin: Walter de Gruyter.

Wright, J. (1989). *Address unknown: The homeless in America.* New York: Walter de Gruyter.

_____ (1990). Homelessness is not healthy for children and other living things. *Child and Youth Services 14*(1):65–88.

Wright, James D., and Joel A. Devine (1992). Counting the homeless: The census bureau's "S-Night" in five U.S. cities. *Evaluation Review 16*(4):355–64.

Wright, James D., and Eleanor Weber (1987). *Homelessness and health.* Washington, DC: McGraw-Hill's Healthcare Information Center.

Ye Qimao (1992). Analysis of demographic trends in small towns in China. Paper presented at the Fifth International Research Conference on Housing, Montreal, Canada, 7–11 July.

Zenzinov, Vladimir (1931). *Deserted: The story of the children abandoned in Soviet Russia.* Trans. Agnes Platt. London: Herbert Joseph. Rpt. Westport, CT: Hyperion, 1975.

Index

Satterthwaite, David, 2, 9
São Paulo (Brazil), 12, 71, 78
Schenk, John, 7, 62
schizophrenia, 31
Scotland, 31, 40
Seattle (Washington), 18, 129
self-help, 108
Senegal, 102
Settlements Information Network
 Africa, 3, 106
sexually exploited, 76, 80
sexually transmitted disease, 48, 78
Shah, P. M., 75, 77, 110
shantytown, 97, 98
shelter, 2–7, 12, 43–48, 75, 83–85,
 89–94, 96, 97, 100, 103, 106,
 107, 109, 112–114, 117, 119,
 121, 123–126, 128
adequate, defined, 4
shelter(s) (homeless), 8–10, 16, 18,
 21, 22, 30, 33–35, 39, 41,
 45–50, 53, 65, 66, 78, 82–84,
 88–93, 106, 109, 112–114, 118,
 121–124
shelter count, 114
sick, 14, 25, 66, 76, 123
sickness, 43, 105
single room occupancy (SRO), 45,
 50, 92
skid row(s), 17, 18, 22, 24, 25, 34,
 36, 46, 87, 128
sleep, 6, 8, 19, 23, 25–27, 29, 31, 51,
 54, 55, 61, 64, 67, 69, 76, 110,
 117, 119, 120
sleep deprivation, 27
sleeping in the rough (sleeping
 rough), 5, 6, 71
slums, 5, 8, 104
S-Night, 112, 114, 115
social networking, 15, 47
social networks, 46, 94, 128
Sokolovsky, Jay, 15, 16, 18, 23, 24,
 127
soup kitchen(s), 1, 15, 24, 27, 35,
 45, 46, 48, 50, 90, 121, 128
Sternberg, David, 3, 15, 84

Spanish, 2, 5, 7, 14, 93
Spradley, James, 22, 128
squatter settlements, 3, 6, 7, 62, 84,
 95, 97, 104, 106, 108
squatters, 62, 90, 98, 100–103, 109,
 119, 123, 129
squatting, 71, 97, 100–103, 119, 122
Sri Lanka, 8
street, 1, 2, 4, 6–8, 11, 12, 18, 21,
 24–26, 30, 32, 35–37, 42–44,
 46, 49, 50, 53–56, 58, 61, 62,
 64, 69, 71–82, 92, 103, 110,
 112–115, 119, 120, 122, 124,
 125, 126, 128, 129
street children, 6, 8, 53–56, 58, 61,
 62, 64, 71–76, 79–82, 124, 125
street count, 114, 115, 119, 122
street educator, 80
street occupations, 25, 26
stress (psychological), 31, 36, 66,
 88, 91
survival, 8, 10, 12, 21–23, 25, 27, 33,
 35, 48, 53, 72, 74, 75, 76, 86,
 97, 124, 127
survival sex, 74, 76
survival strategies, 12, 23, 25, 35,
 48, 74, 97, 124

Taçon, Peter, 58, 60
Taiwan, 26,
Teresina (Brazil), 61
Thailand, 8, 40, 77
Tokyo (Japan), 12, 19
Toronto (Ontario), 36, 37, 50, 69,
 78, 127
transient, 42, 121
tuberculosis (TB), 12, 28, 33, 34, 48,
 90
Turkey, 7
Turner, Bertha, 4
Turner, John, 8, 9, 97

underemployment, 5, 10
unemployment, 10, 16, 19
Undugu (Brotherhood) Society
 (Kenya), 97, 98